EXPERT PR

VOLUME 1

Conversations with Influencers & Innovators

EXPERT PROFILES
VOLUME 1
Conversations with Influencers & Innovators

Featuring

Lisa Charlene Williams

Lauren Bealore

Joy Donnell

Lori Battle

Susan MacNicol

Meagan Ward

Kynia Starkey

Melanie Benson

Dr. Marcy Cole

Nikkia McClain

Dr. Pamela Williamson

Monick Halm

Nicole Neal Armstrong

Authority Media Publishing

Expert Profiles Volume 1 – 1st ed.
ISBN: 978-1-946694-10-2

Royalties from the Retail Sales of *Expert Profiles* are donated to Global Autism Project

AUTISM KNOWS NO BORDERS;
FORTUNATELY NEITHER DO WE.®

Global Autism Project 501(c)3 is a nonprofit organization which provides training to local individuals in evidence-based practices for individuals with autism.

Global Autism Project believes that every child has the ability to learn and their potential should not be limited by geographical bounds.

The Global Autism Project seeks to eliminate the disparity in service provision seen around the world by providing high-quality training to individuals providing services in their local community. This training is made sustainable through regular training trips and contiguous remote training.

You can learn more about the Global Autism Project by visiting GlobalAutismProject.org.

Table of Contents

#Smarthustle #Smartgrind: How Women Can Win in Business and Life Without Working Themselves to Death

"Women are Literally Working Themselves to Death!" This was a recent headline by the Mayo Clinic in 2017 about women. Do you work 40 hours or more? "Long workweeks and copious amounts of stress aren't good for anyone's health, but new research has found that workweeks of 40 hours or more can be especially bad for women," stated the Ohio State University.

Do you sometimes feel like you are in over your head? Have you been struggling to start and grow your business because there is so much to learn, implement and do?

Maybe you're killin' it in business, and you already have a six- or seven-figure income, but at the end of the day, there is not much of you left. Or, maybe you are a woman that has a mission, vision, product, or service that you know people need and you are either a 'best-kept secret' or you're still not yet reaching enough of your ideal prospects that can benefit from what you do.

Female entrepreneurs are the fastest growing group of entrepreneurs right now, and women of color are leading the pack. But did you know that female entrepreneurs (Caucasians) are making on average only $200,000, half of what their male counterparts are making, and that women of color entrepreneurs on average are making less than $40,000 a year?

Statistics show that women entrepreneurs need help growing their revenue, getting funding and obtaining mentorship.

Would you like to know how to hustle and grind the smart way so that it doesn't endanger your health? Do you have any idea if you're on the verge of working yourself to death? Do you know the signs? In this chapter, you will be exposed to how hustling and grinding may be affecting your health and what may be a better way of going about launching, growing and scaling your business.

Conversation with Lisa Charlene Williams

Tell us about the new initiative you have: #SmartHustle #SmartGrind, How Women Can Win in Business and Life Without Working Themselves to Death.

Lisa Williams: Certainly. The #SmartHustle #SmartGrind initiative and program is an all-inclusive marketing campaign specifically for women entrepreneurs, CEOs, & founders that quickly builds know, like and trust, raises their business profile and positions them to attract their ideal customers and clients without working themselves to death!

Most female entrepreneurs, leaders, and business professionals want to make their mark, make more money and still have their me time but are having trouble accomplishing this goal because starting, growing, and scaling a business can come with a lot of stress and can be very time-consuming. There are a lot of options out there and many great professionals to work with but not many, if any at all, that offer a marketing approach that is structured to protect your health, help you quickly establish yourself as the best option and all while establishing you as the Doyenne of your industry, a woman who is the most respected or prominent person in a particular field or industry.

The campaigns we provide women are done for and with them. The internet has opened the door to DIY and leveled the playing field for business owners. You can learn everything you need to be successful. But if you take a moment and think about it, you went into business (whatever your business is) not to become a marketer, not to become a social media maven, not to become a master lead generator or automation expert. So, what has happened now is, everyone is receiving constant marketing, telling you that you must learn this and do that, and if you're honest, it's overwhelming. You should be focused on business practices that allow you to operate in your highest and best use—focusing on sales, marketing, and building relationships.

There is a new book published by a very well-respected professor at the Stanford graduate school of business called *Dying for a Paycheck*. With headlines stating that women are literally working themselves to death and books like *Dying for a Paycheck*, I'm concerned that there are more women than we know whose health is endangered, especially as they are working day in and day out on their business. It appears that women are quietly experiencing health challenges (some suffering in silence) and may not be correlating these challenges to the hustling and grinding and long hours they are working.

That is a very good point. So, how do you help women win?

The #SmartHustle #SmartGrind initiative and program is structured to help women win in business and life. It allows women to start, run, grow and scale their business without having to compete to succeed and without having to work 50–60 hours to build a successful, scalable and sustainable business, which can be very dangerous for their health according to Allard Dembe, professor of health services management at Ohio State University. The link between long work hours and disease "seems to be present a bit in men but is tremendously more evident in women." When the study compared women who worked 30 to 40 hours a week to those who worked more than 60 hours a week, women who worked more had substantially higher rates of disease. Women who worked 60 or more hours had more than three times the risk of heart disease, non-skin cancer, and diabetes.

I'd like to also share some of the top challenges many female entrepreneurs are facing today while starting, growing and scaling their businesses. Tell me if you can relate to any of these:

- You're going at it alone and are probably a one-woman show
- You've had to work harder to get the respect and recognition you deserve
- You make less than $200,000, and as a woman of color, you make less than $40,000 in annual revenue
- You're working more than 40 hours a week
- You don't give yourself the credit you deserve or share your success
- You tend to overextend yourself and don't relinquish or delegate well
- You lack female mentors that look like you, and you probably don't have access to mentors at all
- You don't have the credit, savings, or resources to get funding
- You fear failure, so you don't take calculated risk to grow your business
- You are working so hard to make the right move in your business; you don't invest in your personal development, a coach, or hiring a consultant. So, you stay on the hamster wheel, and the needle doesn't move in your business

As you see, in addition to the stress and challenges, there are also health risks associated with working long hours, which women tend to face on the road to success. It is, therefore, important for women to consider how they are going about running their businesses.

What are the advantages of evaluating the number of hours we are putting into our businesses?

Lisa Williams: Great question, because we don't typically think about evaluating how the amount of time we are spending working might be affecting our overall wellbeing. We tend to look at our work and health separately.

So, taking time to look at your business from a wellness perspective can help prevent a potential illness, disease, diagnosis—and honestly, death. A Japanese woman worked 159 hours of overtime, took only two days off in the month, and it led up to her death from heart failure in July 2013. Taking a moment to stop and think about how many hours you are putting in every day and week after week and reading up on how that can adversely affect your health could be lifesaving. And hopefully, after reading this chapter, more women will be encouraged to evaluate their hustling and grinding and the possible toll their business could be having on their health.

I hope that my chapter becomes a wake-up call for women that stirs them to evaluate what they may be risking in their effort to grow that business and reach a pinnacle of success. You may be making good money, but eventually … at what cost?

What are some of the biggest myths about what a successful business is?

Lisa Williams: First, I want to say that success for men can look very different than success for women. Success for men tends to involve competition, working long hours, outworking their competition, and making a ton of money. For women, success can look and feel much different. Women tend to want to have a business that makes a difference in some way; that is important to us. We also tend to not just want success in our business but in our overall lives. For many women, personal time and family time can be just as important as our success in business. Typically, competition doesn't feel as good to women as it does to men (collaboration feels better), and though we, too, want to make oodles of money, typically, not at the expense of our joy and happiness.

What are some common misconceptions about what women entrepreneurs must do to become successful in business?

Lisa Williams: Some misconceptions I have heard are:

- That you have to compete to succeed
- That staying on the grind is what evidentially will make you grow
- That you must network and be everywhere
- That you have to learn and constantly be on all the social media platforms

Let me share some quick stories about some health scares some successful women have faced over the last few years.

We constantly hear about self-care and the work-life balance, but what about the hustle and grind? Arianna Huffington, the founder of *The Huffington Post*, had a wakeup call; she fell asleep at her desk and woke up in a pool of blood at her desk. During her doing-it-all period of working 18-hour days, she was so run down she collapsed, and she broke her nose from exhaustion.

Maria Menounos recently quit her job as the E! News host, and after a brain tumor diagnoses and having surgery, she said, "I am going to be still for a bit and see what I'm supposed to be in the world." Wendy Williams, the TV show host, took a three-week hiatus after passing out on national television and revealed that she has Graves' disease and said, "We take care of everyone else but ourselves, and I'm not doing that anymore. Wendy first." In 2015, Kate Walsh was working 80 hours a week and learned that she had a benign brain tumor. She said that women tend to put others' needs before their own. Solange, Beyoncé's sister, had to cancel her New Year's Eve concert because she had been dealing with an autonomic disorder and couldn't perform. Iyanla Vanzant, of Fix My Life, couldn't speak at the Essence Festival in 2016 due to a health scare and said, "I'm very clear that my experience was a warning."

If this can happen to women who have achieved high levels of financial success, with all the resources and support they have, what might hustling and grinding be doing to you? Women really need to take the work-life balance serious! We (women) are made different and should structure our life with that consideration in mind. We show women a smarter way to hustle and grind that includes collaboration and leverage so their preserving and protecting their health is added into the business strategy.

What are some of the most common fears women business owners face different from men?

Lisa Williams: Again, going back to some of the challenges we discussed earlier, some of them double also as fears many women have. The fear of failure, the fear of not being successful and having to quit and go back to work, the fear of people knowing that you weren't successful. The fear and wonder of "Am I in over my head?" And lastly, the fear of "Will I ever achieve the vision and plan I have for my life and business?"

The concern I don't know if women think about enough is, how much stress they may be under and how dangerous eliminating their 'me time' can be.

How can they get past these fears?

Lisa Williams: The short answer ... working smarter, not harder. By implementing more efficient and effective structures, systems, and automations, they will quickly see that the stress will begin to melt off them.

What other obstacles do you see that might be preventing female entrepreneurs from having six- and seven-figure businesses?

Lisa Williams: Oh, there are many. It is proven that women don't get funding, therefore making it almost impossible to scale to high six and seven figures in a time frame that many male entrepreneurs can.

Another big obstacle is not having mentors, not having access to women modeling, women in your same line of business who are already successful not only telling you what you should do but you actually being able to see what they are doing.

What are some little-known pitfalls or common mistakes you see female entrepreneurs make as they hustle and grind their way to growing and scaling their businesses?

Lisa Williams: I would say being a solo entrepreneur, not hiring a coach, and not utilizing co-working spaces. Also, not realizing that investing in your own personal development is key. These three investments alone can increase growth and sales quickly while protecting you from burnout.

How can these pitfalls/mistakes be avoided?

Lisa Williams: Much of this can be avoided by considering 'marketing differently.' Today, a real estate agent knocked on my door. He was doing what he has been taught to do—a marketing approach that has been successful over the years for real estate agents. Most industries have marketing approaches that still work, but today, with the internet and social media leveraged correctly, you can avoid some of the traditional marketing approaches and implement some that are less taxing and more effective. Pull marketing is the new strategy. I urge women especially to consider marketing differently by incorporating pull marketing which draws their ideal client to them instead of seeking clients. By leveraging relationships, platforms, and the media, and using attraction marketing tactics to draw your ideal customers and clients, you will have to do less and less hustling and grinding.

Can you share an example of how you have helped a woman overcome these obstacles with the #smarthustle #smartgrind approach?

Lisa Williams: Yes, I worked with a woman who struggled to get clients. She said she knew her services could help people, but she felt like a 'best-kept secret,' and she didn't enjoy selling. She participated in one of our collaborative book projects with other professionals, much like this book. Collaborating in a project like this immediately enhances your credibility, strengthens your business profile and builds buzz around what you do.

After the book was published and reached best-seller status, she told me that now, she just sends a copy of her book before she meets with her prospects, and she no longer has to sell herself, and the meetings are totally different now. She doesn't have to spend time promoting her accomplishments, and sometimes, her prospects are already pre-sold and ready to work with her.

What inspired you to lead the charge for women and blow the whistle on the hustle and grind?

Lisa Williams: Several things inspired me. The quote that "Women are literally working themselves to death" was one. Learning that women entrepreneurs are the fastest growing group but are struggling the most and making less than half of what their male counterparts make. And lastly, learning that women of color entrepreneurs are making on average under $40,000 a year, I said to myself, "Not on my watch."

But the biggest reason was my own health challenge (that I am currently walking through) and my own journey of starting and growing a new business and the stress that has come with it the second time around.

Can you share a lesson you learned early on that still impacts how you do business today?

Lisa Williams: I learned early on that sticking with something and working hard will not in itself make you successful. There is a lot more involved in achieving success.

What are the most important questions female entrepreneurs should ask themselves to ensure that they are not on the verge of working themselves to death?

Lisa Williams: I would say to ask yourself:

- Am I working 10–12-hour days on a regular basis and then coming home and cooking, cleaning, and tending to my family?
- Am I carving out my me time (whatever that is), or have I been forgoing my me time?
- Have I seen a difference in my stamina and my overall health since I started my business?

These are a few questions to start with.

What should women in business, thought leaders, and women in general consider when they are defining what winning is?

Lisa Williams: First, I would say, ask yourself, what is winning for you? Another question would be, *If I'm winning in business and not in my personal life, do I still consider that winning?*

I love to get the dictionary definition of words because, many times, we think we know the definition, but many times, you get a fresh perspective when you look a word up. Winning means "manage to succeed or achieve something by effort, acquire or secure as a result of an endeavor."

So, think about what winning in business is for you; is quality of life and good health a part of that?

What would you like to leave women with to think about as they are working in and on their business day to day?

Lisa Williams: First, I believe if you are reading this chapter, there is a reason, and you must be walking in or approaching your winning season. Secondly, I hope that my chapter informed you and inspired you to think about how the way you are going about starting, growing, and scaling your business might be affecting you in ways you may not have considered. And, I would say to a woman who is going at her business alone, can you really keep going at this pace? I would say to a woman who has successfully scaled her business to also consider what I have shared today. I would say to a woman who is determined and out there grinding, working 50–60 hours a week, who may be going home and working the 2nd shift (which is considered the time you spend taking care of your family), to please consider what we have talked about and take measures to prioritize your health.

Lastly, I hope that any woman reading this chapter can be honest with herself and is willing to take a look and see if you are exhausted at the end of most days, see if you have started scaling back on your self-care or your me time and if you have noticed health challenges or signs. Don't only go to the doctor; have a business check-up as well.

I want women to know that there is a program available, designed specifically with them in mind, so you can have the business and life you desire without working night and day, without having to compete and without working yourself to death. I also want women to think about where they are, where they are headed, and how they want their life to look in five years, and not just from a financial standpoint but also from a quality of life perspective, because we don't really think about how something can affect our quality of life until something happens.

Finally, if you feel that it is truly your time to win, I mean win in a way that lights you up, and you are willing to disrupt what you've been taught or what you believe is the way to market and grow your business, I encourage you to check out the #smarthustle smartgrind for women. I know I can position you faster than you can position yourself to make your mark, make more money and get back your me time.

How can someone find out more about you, Lisa, and the #SmartHustle #SmartGrind initiative and program for women?

Lisa Williams: They can visit www.SmartHustleSmartGrind.com.

They can also download our checklist to make sure that they are not on the verge of working themselves to death at amiontheverge.com.

About Lisa Charlene Williams

Lisa Charlene Williams is the founder of Smart Hustle Publishing and the Smart Hustle Agency. Her specialty is to build greater know, like, and trust for her clients and help them succeed in business and life. Williams is an exposure specialist, publisher, radio show producer and best-selling author. She helps entrepreneurs leverage what she calls the new 9 P's of marketing—positioning, publishing, publicity, public speaking, platforms, partnerships, and personal social responsibility, processes and preservation—to grow their business, establish their expert platform and create the life and business they desire.

Lisa Williams is the visionary of the #SmartHustle #SmartGrind initiative and program, and she is on a mission to help women become the Doyennes of their industry, the most respected or prominent people in any particular field, and to stop women from working themselves to death.

She has been featured in hundreds of media outlets, including ABC, CBS, NBC, and FOX affiliates, and she and her colleagues have helped over 300 professionals become best-selling authors. Lisa has personally helped 22 professionals publish books and reach best-selling status. Several of her publishing campaigns have reached best-selling status next to industry giants such as Amazon CEO Jeff Bezos, Facebook CEO Sheryl Sandberg's popular book *Lean In*, and the legendary basketball star Michael Jordan's book.

Lisa Williams has been in media and marketing for over 25 years. In her early career, she worked for the *Los Angeles Daily News* and was the liaison to the major sports teams such as the Los Angeles Lakers, Clippers, Sparks, Kings, Dodgers and Avengers. She has also worked with brands such as Disney on Ice, the Boys and Girls Club, and the YMCA. Lisa Williams received a basketball scholarship to U.C. Berkeley, has a degree in Economics. She is a Christian and a single mother of two who prides herself on providing resources and exposure to help people live a better quality of life.

WEBSITE
SmartHustleAgency.com

FACEBOOK
Facebook.com/smarthustleagencyFacebook.com/smarthustles martgrind

TWITTER
Twitter.com/SmartHustleGrind

LINKEDIN
LinkedIn.com/in/LisaWilliams818

You Can Be a Part of Changing the Narrative for Women of Color in Entrepreneurship and Business

What do you envision when you think of a successful entrepreneur? Are they black, white, male, or female? How are they viewed by their colleagues and society? There are many common narratives for women of color in the business world today. Some are positive, and some are, well, not so much. Would you like your business, mission, and contribution to the world to impact the current narratives that exist for women of color? Do you have an idea or business that you just can't seem to get off the ground or figure out where to even start? You might have exceptional leadership skills but are unsure of how to make a name for yourself in a world that does not have many business role models for women of color. Do you desire to have your own community that can help you thrive and understand the resources and support that you need?

Y.A.B. has three areas of focus—business development, community engagement & mentorship, and personal development.

Through the combination of these different pillars, you receive specific tools and guidance to start a business as a woman of color. You will find that you don't need a huge financial investment or fancy marketing when you begin to tap into all this organization has to offer. You will get the pushing and encouragement you need to go far while gaining partners in the community.

Think about the world twenty years from now. Do you think there will be more women of color in politics, in Fortune 500 companies or paving the way for new industries? Or will the business landscape stay the same? All it takes is a leap of faith to step out of the 'norm' and decide to make a change. You could be the entrepreneur that inspires a new generation of women of color to design a whole new life. If you want more insight into this new movement that Y.A.B. has created, I know you'll find the interview with Lauren Bealore enlightening. —Conversation with Lisa C. Williams

Lisa Charlene Williams is the Founder of the #SmartHustle #SmartGrind movement (amiontheverge.com), an initiative to help female entrepreneurs succeed in business and life, stop working themselves to death and become the Doyennes of their industry, a woman who is the most respected or prominent person in a particular field.

Conversation with Lauren Bealore

What is Young, Ambitious and Beautiful, and what support do you provide women of color?

Lauren Bealore: Young, Ambitious and Beautiful, which is abbreviated Y.A.B., is an organization that operates as a venture conglomerate created by myself and my co-founders, Courtney Griffin and Brittany Daisy Colston. In 2012, a year from our undergraduate experience at Michigan State University, we thought there was a need for change regarding women and how they were received, not only in the media but also in the workplace. At that time, we saw a lot of millennial women gaining a lot of ground with start-ups that they were creating, but they weren't gaining the publicity they needed. A lot of men who owned start-ups were receiving much notoriety and investments from venture capitalists, but women, especially women of color, were not receiving funding. That was really the premise for why we started Y.A.B.

As professional women, as well as venture partners, we wanted to have several businesses and put them in a Chamber of Commerce type of structure. When we started, we were operating like Procter and Gamble or Johnson and Johnson, large companies which own several businesses that operate under one umbrella. Technically, each business has its own CEO and its own founder. Even when you look at a city's Chamber of Commerce, it has different businesses that are housed under it, and those businesses are provided resources by the Chamber of Commerce. That's the model of how we wanted to do our program. We wanted to bring that kind of mindset to a community for women of color because we don't usually operate like that. We usually operate individually, and we want to break that stereotype.

What would you say are the three areas you help with under the Y.A.B. structure?

Lauren Bealore: The Y.A.B. structure is broken down into three different entities, one for each co-founder; that way, we never have to compete on which initiatives we want to take on. We can draw from three different personalities with three different missions but are inclined to one.

I operate under business development, which is my forte, especially coming from the industry I come from. My first co-founder operates under community engagement mentorship. She builds all partnerships with schools. She got a partnership with a Chicago public school where we were given a school by the school district. My second co-founder operates under personal development where she focuses on self-care initiatives. She created the Y.A.B. book club and operates that.

Again, with my entity, I partner with a lot of different resources and a lot of funding and management programs so women do not have to seek out loans for their start-ups. I partner with corporations so women do not have to try to find brick and mortar because that's a cause for more input rather than output. That's where I step in and make sure we get good partnerships—so that with each entity, women are able to get the best kind of results for themselves and their business.

What are some of the advantages you feel in changing the narratives for women of color? How would it help us?

Lauren Bealore: Oh, it would help in tons of ways. Excellent question. One of the advantages to aiding women of color in changing this narrative is that you don't have to address the DEI issue anymore, which is a huge passion of mine. We're still trying to answer the question of what diversity, equity and inclusion looks like, but we are asking those who are not people of color, whether they're in education, corporate, or entrepreneurship. We're asking the question, but why are we asking those who aren't people of color? If you put people of color in leadership positions, they would make sure that they create platforms where they are able to include minorities in organizations. As a starter, I think if we change that narrative, we don't have to keep addressing the same issues, or to say it less professionally, we don't have to continuously ask white people what they can do for us.

I also think we can change what the future of the community looks like. Until we can change what successful entrepreneurs look like, we'll continue to have whites in top positions, and people of color will never be considered. It's okay to start out with a start-up as a side business and still have your 9−5 job which helps pay for that start-up business. There's absolutely nothing wrong with that. The problem, however, is that if you're not looking at your start-up as eventually being a sole business for yourself, then you will never reap the full rewards of that business.

Until that mindset is changed, there's really nothing you can do when you see white women or white men, especially in the tech industry, go into business. They go into business with the mindset that their start-up will eventually be paying bills, be creating a legacy and be the foundation for their career. People of color do not necessarily think that way. So, until they change the way they think, they will continue to be treated like a by-product.

What do you feel are the biggest myths out there that you would like to see change for women of color?

Lauren Bealore: For starters, one of the myths that I would like to see change is that we are particularly accustomed to working in certain industries like the hair care industry or the make-up industry. That being said, those are not the only industries that women of color can launch start-ups in. To be honest, however, if women of color do come to venture capitalists and investors with a unique idea, if they do not feel like the Black community, which is the target audience, will benefit from it or if they think they don't have use for it, they're not going to make an investment. I know this because I have a friend who works in the advertising industry who has told me of times when she has been the only woman of color in the room for a well-known Black brand but was told by non-Black people what they think Black women want to wear or what they want to receive from the brand.

It's very important that women of color change the myth of the type of businesses they want to start in order to change the myth of the kind of jobs they are willing to invest in.

Another myth that we definitely need to change is that we don't know how to partner with not only people of the same demographics but also people of different demographics. One thing that we have done with Y.A.B., which I am super proud of, is, we have partnered with many businesses and organizations that people typically think they're gentrifying to bring awareness that there are businesses out there that you can take over.

What would you say are the common fears that women of color have as they start their business?

Lauren Bealore: The first fear I often hear that women of color have is regarding funding. People believe you have to have a certain amount of money to start. We did not start Y.A.B. with a large sum of money. We kept thinking smart. I don't think we spent money since year three of founding, and we've been running for six years.

One of my co-founders designed our logo. As far as publicity, I did outreach to over 70 organizations. I did it all. I've never hired a public relations person. Everything we've done is homegrown. Sometimes, you just have to Google how to teach yourself new things you need to do. We also used the power of social media to spread the word about our program. Now, it has really grown and taken on a life of its own. People think their website needs to look a certain way. It does need to be professional, but you don't have to spend a lot of money to get it to look that way. When you are just starting up, spending a lot of money is not realistic. You take what talent and resources you have and get the job done.

The first thing you do is create a mission. You can't thrive if you don't have a mission statement. We tell this to people who want to work with us because we are very particular with those we work with. I have a lot of people who want to partner with me, but I don't even know what their mission is. How can you successfully target a demographic for your business if you don't have a mission for who you want to target?

What are some little-known pitfalls or common errors that you see women of color make on the road to growing their business?

Lauren Bealore: One of the biggest is the copycat syndrome of trying to create a business similar to other ones. We have not seen that a lot with Y.A.B., but I have seen a lot of this from other people. I'm noticing it because it's like a trend where a lot of people's brand all look the same. That's why we wanted our logo to be different. When we started in 2012, I noticed there was a similarity in color among businesses run by women of color. I know this is going to sound weird, but non-people of color think using pink and black is being Black. I hate to say it, but it looks quite bad when people come to us. I may not work with those who use pink and black—because they think that's the kind of color we want to see, and it's not. That's a big pitfall.

If you don't want to pay for something, then I suggest doing some Google research on what appeals to the eye of an investor. Don't do something that will catch the eye of your demographic because if it's a good business or idea, they're going to follow through anyway. Design with investors in mind because those are the people who will pay for your funding and partner with you.

A lot of people go into press these days, but I saw recently where *The Huffington Post* stopped allowing people to do opinion articles. Thank God! Everyone was starting to say things like, "I write for *The Huffington Post*" or "I had a feature with *The Huffington Post*." Such sayings weren't true. I'm not saying doing so was bad, but I think it was smart of *The Huffington Post* to stop doing that because people were building public relations on it. A lot of people depend on free social media advertising and press. I often say that you haven't made it until you can be nationally recognized and the features come to you. It wasn't until we got to NBC News that I saw the power of old-school media.

Our NBC News piece went out nationally. I would Google our names, and all these news articles would come up because people would steal the story from other people. At the end, you'll end up having credit that you didn't ask for. People underestimate the power of that.

I'm from Michigan. Even when you are looking at Detroit, it's a big city small town, and a lot of people think that the local press can catapult their careers. But in looking at my career, it's the national press that took me to new heights.

I guess I should explain that more. If you are posting things to the local press to get people to come out and learn, I think that works. But if you are building a larger platform, then you use the local press to get to the national press. That's what I'm trying to say. We've used both, and it's been great.

Can you give us a success story of women you have helped overcome challenges?

Lauren Bealore: There is one woman who wanted to launch a start-up and write a book. I told her, "Okay, you've got to go for it." She didn't necessarily think it was the right time. I said, "There is no perfect time. Your business is like a relationship. You are going to have good and bad times." So, basically, the testimony is that she started last year.

What inspired you to become an advocate for women of color?

Lauren Bealore: I would say what inspires me is that I am a stereotype kind of person. I am content with being the first and not the last. I live my life bouncing in an intersection alley, where I'm bouncing both my gender and race to better serve in leadership positions. Intersection alley was first coined by a woman of color, which is something a lot of people don't know. It is more like a duo consciousness. I'm reminded of Richard Wright's book, *Black Boy*, where he talks about duo consciousness and the veil that comes with it. My job is to lift that veil.

I have to be honest, there was not much forethought that went into doing what I'm doing now. Coming out of the womb as a woman and as a black person was the inspiration. I have had some experiences, not as harsh as others, but I've seen both sides of the coin. As Shirley Wilson said, "I don't do the whimpering and complaining. I don't have a startling experience. It was just me being black."

Can you share a lesson that you learned while doing business?

Lauren Bealore: Sometimes, people align with you when it benefits them. I had a situation once when I got a television appearance for an organization that we were collaborating with. It was our outreach that got the appearance, and they wanted to be included on television. We said, "No, we are going to talk about it on air for you, but you are not going on air."

Long story short, the lesson there is that you are going to get the opportunity. Either take it or pass it along, because you can't combine the two. So, make sure your partnership is good. I think that sort of sums it up.

How can each of us individually change the narrative? How can we as women of color change the narrative? What is just one nugget you can share?

Lauren Bealore: Start taking more chances in leadership. I think if we start taking more chances, we will be making sure we put ourselves in positions to reach diverse opportunities out of our comfort zone.

What's the most important thing that a woman of color can do to change the narrative?

Lauren Bealore: There's a quote that can answer that question. It says, "We cannot break down the barriers within society without first breaking down the barriers within ourselves." Once the barriers in your person are broken down individually, that's the only way you can carry out a change in narrative or a change in movement for that matter.

What would you like to leave women with about the importance of changing that narrative and why Y.A.B. can help?

Lauren Bealore: I would like to leave women with the idea that in order to have a seat at the table, you have to know the building that the table is in. This means that you keep your eyes open for power structures. If you understand how power works, you will be successful in life. Understanding the power structures is the only way of breaking them down. Y.A.B. would leave you with our understanding of how power works. We are constantly providing resources to make sure you have a seat at the table.

About Lauren Bealore

As a Michigan State University graduate with a Bachelor of Arts in Social Relations and Policy, Lauren Bealore has set herself up to have a background that can flourish in multiple areas. Her student-led leadership experience, coupled with the internship experience with the Michigan Democratic Party, helped to solidify her consistent pursuit of the law and government realm.

Lauren decided to utilize her degree to further pursue a Master of Arts in Public Policy from The New England College. She continued her career in the Finance Department of political campaigns, beginning on the Congressional Campaign of the 14th District of Michigan as Assistant Finance Director and then on to be the Finance Director for a Democratic Nominee for the 39th District for the Michigan House of Representatives. In total, she helped to raise $800,000 in campaign elections in 2014, being the only Millennial African American woman in Michigan working in the fundraising realm of politics.

Currently, Lauren is the Corporate Relations and Events Manager for the Michigan League of Conservation Voters, taking her fundraising efforts to the Environmental Policy area of politics. In February 2015, she was appointed as Commissioner for the City of Southfield's Total Living Commission and was elected First Vice Chair of the Commission.

Her role with Y.A.B. is to be the driving force behind the business and development entity of Y.A.B. She has a passion for helping to develop businesses for women of color and to further promote the businesses that already exist. Her personal career in politics, working with several corporate executives and business owners as campaign donors, has helped to expand the Y.A.B. network. Through the business development entity of Y.A.B., she works with co-working spaces to change the narrative and bring more women of color to their resources to create collaborations and opportunity. By fostering event collaborations and outreach to several female-owned businesses, she helps to further flourish and carry out the Y.A.B. mission.

WEBSITE
iamyab.org

FACEBOOK
Facebook.com/iamyab

INSTAGRAM
Instagram.com/iamyab

LINKEDIN
LinkedIn.com/in/LaurenBealore

Every Woman Needs to See Self-Care as a Leadership Skill to Reach Her Purpose and Achieve Her Dream Life

What is your legacy? It's not how much money you make, how many buildings you design, or how big your house is. Take a moment and think, *When I'm no longer here, what lives will I have touched?* That's your legacy. Having a strong philosophy and vision for your business to make an impact is what is going to draw your ideal clients to you. Protecting your brand and mission is of utmost importance in growing your business and creating that legacy for generations to come.

Self-care is a key component in being an outstanding leader. Learning when to stop and take care of you is going to prevent mistakes, provide clarity and help you focus on what's most important to your business. By becoming clear on the philosophy and mission behind what you are doing, you will be able to create the images, promotions, media, and marketing that is true to what you stand for.

Do you really know the core values behind what you do, or have you strayed from that? Consider how you want your brand to be perceived in the public eye. Do you think it's relatable to the people you want to attract? These are all things that can help you succeed in your growth and leadership. At the end of the day, you will be amazed at what you can accomplish by just getting humble and owning who you are. If you want more information on how you can achieve this, I know you'll find Joy Donnell's interview enlightening. −Conversation with Lisa C. Williams

Lisa Charlene Williams is the Founder of the #SmartHustle #SmartGrind movement (amiontheverge.com), an initiative to help female entrepreneurs succeed in business and life, stop working themselves to death and become the Doyennes of their industry, a woman who is the most respected or prominent person in a particular field.

Conversation with Joy Donnell

Share about your role with the Vanichi Magazine, your mission and your charge to women to look at self-care as a leadership skill.

Joy Donnell: Vanichi was building a luxury brand, and I had luxury branding expertise. I came and spoke to them about how to make content that would help the brand grow in the right way and showed them how to better understand their audience and their needs. I ended up becoming a part of the company. I started off as COO, and now I'm CEO and editor-in-chief.

My mission and charge to women is to look at self-care as a leadership skill. First, I highly recommend that women start taking ownership of their self-care. In my opinion, self-care is not just sleeping, drinking water, and exercising; it's also community building. It's a holistic journey.

Self-care is treating the whole human that you are. That means you need camaraderie with people who are going to challenge you in the right way, challenge you to grow and challenge you to step up. They will also body-check you when you are not doing what you're supposed to be doing. Self-care is being able to have downtime and let creativity flow to you. It's all the things that will help you grow into the exact leader that you're supposed to be and the best version of the human being that you were placed here to be.

Combining luxury, leadership, and self-care allows you to start getting what you should get, along with exactly what you are looking for. It's a very different way to move through the world.

What would you say are the advantages of women changing how they view leadership with regard to their self-care?

Joy Donnell: I think one of the advantages of women seeing self-care as a leadership skill is that it cultivates better mental health for them. I don't think that power corrupts. Isolation is what corrupts. I have found that women make decisions within a bubble or get so low in their journey they are convinced that they are the only one. They think that they are on an island by themselves and they cannot rely on anyone else. No one is going to help them, and if someone does come on board to help, they're going to derail everything. Many women feel that they must carry the load by themselves, so they end up making decisions within that bubble. Either way, that's a path towards self-destruction. It's not a path towards health for your mind, for your body, and for your spirit.

What do you feel are the biggest myths out there when it comes to an accomplished woman prioritizing her self-care?

Joy Donnell: I think that many women are caught up with looking like they are incredibly busy all the time. To some extent, I think we have glorified busyness. It has turned into a competition among women to see who is the busiest, who has the least amount of time to even know what they're thinking. Our male counterparts, on the other hand, take their downtime. Many men have a regular boys' night out, but women often remain home with the kids and never take time off for themselves. I remind women that they must take a break from their children and doing so doesn't make them a horrible person.

Women need to give themselves the permission to take a break and not work themselves to death. We cannot keep running ourselves into the ground. Unfortunately, however, women are not very kind to one another. I have seen women come back to the workplace after taking time off and be attacked with attitude and vitriol by other women.

What are some common misconceptions about a luxury lifestyle and success for women?

Joy Donnell: I think we as women have been given a wrong definition of what a luxury lifestyle is. Most have been taught that it's all about stuff, and the person with the most stuff at the end of life wins. That's not true. We don't own anything. We are just stewards of everything that we have. When you move your thinking away from the ownership idea to a stewardship perspective, it alleviates a lot of stress and strain for you. When you stop thinking that you must spend an exorbitant amount of money to gain a status symbol so people will bow down to you, then things will shift.

What are some of the most common fears women have regarding their confidence and assertiveness as they try to balance leadership and self-care?

Joy Donnell: What I've noticed most in the work I've done with women is that when they are in a leadership role, their main fear is not being seen—and not being seen properly.

It's not so much: "Oh, no. The spotlight is on me. Let me shrink from the spotlight." It's more of: "When the spotlight gets shined on me, what are others going to see? Are they going to see me or are they going to bastardize and warp my image and words?" Several studies have been done that show that when women are forceful and passionate in group discussions, they're seen as angry and a bitch. But when men are forceful and passionate in group discussions, they might still be seen as being a little angry, but they are more positively tolerated because they are seen as being strong and steadfast.

When a woman starts being forceful in a room, it can sound like she's disappointed. That disappointment is probably going to make people attack her, which in turn will make her defensive. Women can curtail that by using language that first states their intention and their purpose before getting into why something annoys the crap out of them. They can completely change a conversation by saying, "It really does feel like we've been talking about this for two months and we still haven't accomplished anything." Or they can say, "This is something I'm very passionate about because I've been battling this for five years and I've seen the detriment that it's done to people and to communities. We cannot keep letting time go by. I propose we do this." Men actually start to hear you within that conversation. The tone and the presentation take them off the defense.

The fear of not being seen properly and of not being validated properly can be overcome by using the right language.

What other perceived obstacles do you see that might be preventing women from owning their power?

Joy Donnell: For lack of another way to put it, a lot of times, we are defeated by hallucinations. When I say that, I mean I hear so many people saying, "Oh my goodness, I want to be out there, but I don't want to be famous in the way that people are going through my trash. I don't want to be like

Angelina Jolie. I want to be able to go down the street." My response is that you're holding yourself back from something that has yet to happen.

This is an example of someone being defeated by a hallucination in their head. Don't focus on what you don't want to happen. We can actually immobilize ourselves over something that we don't want to happen, possibly, eventually or perhaps in the unforeseeable future.

Let's talk about things that prevent women from succeeding. What would you say are some pitfalls or common mistakes you've seen women make on the road to climbing the corporate ladder or growing their business?

Joy Donnell: As they're climbing, I've seen a lot of women lose the sense of themselves and even lose what their original motivation was for what they were doing. This is because they give in to the fear, the pressure, and the negativity that is around them. I do work with my clients on how to take that negativity and use it as momentum towards the positive goal that they had in the first place.

Can you share an example of how you have helped a woman overcome an obstacle in her business with your luxury approach to branding?

Joy Donnell: There's a fashion brand that I worked with, whose owner was very artistic, but she was not giving her brand and her collections an opportunity to grow and be seen properly. She was holding herself back from dealing with celebrities, and she was doing so out of fear. It wasn't so much the fear that she thought a celebrity would blow her brand up and she wouldn't be able to fulfill the order. She was scared that a celebrity would override or overtake her brand. I started having conversations with her to find out what made her think that celebrities would come in and just take over her business.

We found that she felt she had to go after the same celebrity that everyone else was going after. She was thinking, *I've got to use this celebrity or that celebrity, even though they're not the kind of celebrity I want with my brand.* I asked her a simple question: "What celebrities do you want with your brand?" She said to me, "I don't think anyone has ever asked me that question."

I then basically showed her a path to dealing with the type of celebrities she wanted to interact with and how she could build partnerships with them. She started doing business with those type of celebrities, and it changed everything about her visibility.

What inspired you to do the work you do?

Joy Donnell: Failure is what inspires me. I was in college when someone suggested PR to me as a career path. I thought it was the worst idea I had ever heard in my life, and the person who made the suggestion was someone I respected. But the idea of PR repelled me. I said, "I don't know anyone in my family who has done any type of PR." My father expected me to have a real career. I was fixated on international law, so I went back to school and began working on a social action campaign that changed my life. I failed miserably at the social action campaign, and that's the failure that propelled me to learn PR. I changed my compass from corporate PR (which is where I started) to entertainment and luxury PR.

I realized that I wanted to use media as a tool to increase our humanity. I now combine everything that I understand about publicity, branding, content strategy, and the distribution of that content through the media. I understand it from both sides—from the PR side as well as the editorial side of the process. I understand what editors are looking for. I know how to craft messaging that really helps people break through the noise.

That's how everything culminated for me. I also have a personal passion to foster female entrepreneurship because I know that when you invest in women, women invest in their communities. I focused on fashion because fashion is one of the biggest industries on the planet. It's one of the biggest polluters as well as one of the biggest employers.

I am very selective about who I work with. I'm not for anyone and everyone. I'm very targeted, and what I do, I do fiercely and relentlessly. That's how my career has evolved into who I am and what I do now.

Is there a lesson you learned early on that still impacts how you do business today?

Joy Donnell: There are several. But the one I will share is this: "I do not talk about big ideas with people who have small minds." To me, that is how you exhaust yourself. I have come to realize that when you have a lot of power, it is reckless of you and irresponsible of you to leave your house without that power being driven by intent.

I was lucky enough to find the space to sit down, check myself and get back to what my actual focus was. Sharing big ideas with people with small minds will quickly exhaust you. Unfortunately, I did that early on, and it showed up in my life and was a wake-up call. I messed up my thyroid. I had allowed myself to get exhausted from working. I didn't think I deserved to have what I should have.

Long story short, I realized that I lacked gratitude. I did not fully realize what was around me or what was available to me. I had misinterpreted everything in my life. I was looking at it from a place of lack and not realizing the abundance. I had to tap into that abundance mindset that I had been taught growing up by my parents. I had not realized my blessing, but when I started to realize it, my entire world shifted for me.

What's the most important question women should ask themselves as they take inventory of their goals, their self-care, their leadership and their legacy?

Joy Donnell: I know it sounds simple, but I think that it is important for a woman to sit down and ask herself, *What is my intention?* and not just *What is my purpose?* What is it that she is seeking to do? What is the intention behind that? What is getting her out of bed in the morning? What is her motivation? Oftentimes, the answer will be a myriad of things. It won't just be one thing but several things that feed into a central idea of something you want to give to this world or some way you want to leave an impact.

What would you like to share to help a woman better incorporate their intention into their message and mission?

Joy Donnell: I would say to do daily checks of intention. We tend to think that things are permanent. But things are always changing, and we are highly adaptable. Because of being highly adaptable, you constantly get different stimuli.

You experience new things. You grow. The world will try to shrink you, and because of that, you must check in with your intention every day.

About Joy Donnell

Joy Donnell is a brand and content strategist, activist and entrepreneur driven by purpose. She believes in owning your power, and for Donnell, power is you owning your voice, image, influence, and intentions. Her vision is to create media that increases humanity. Donnell also scours the globe for unique, handcrafted couture pieces from emerging designers of diverse backgrounds to help expand culture through luxury markets.

Her PR expertise touches all her work as she brings that insight to content strategy, content creation, and luxury fashion and lifestyle branding. When she isn't behind the camera creating fashion editorials and fashion films as a producer or director, she steps in front of the camera as a model and sustainable luxury advocate. Donnell is currently the CEO of Parajin Media Corp and Editor-in-Chief of its flagship luxury lifestyle publication, *Vanichi*. She also serves as an Advisor for The Geekie Awards, Creative Visions Foundation and Charles and Company.

As an international speaker, Donnell loves to share her knowledge about branding, multiplatform content, and public image. Alongside Nzinga Blake, Donnell recently guest lectured at UCLA's School of Film, Television and Digital Media on that very subject matter. Her eBook, *Pitch Perfect*, is a quick guide on establishing brand and PR best practices for the motivated entrepreneur. The book has sold widely around the world.

Donnell is currently curating rising luxury brands from emerging economies to feature in her work with *Vanichi*. You can also find her sharing these discoveries on *HuffPost*.

WEBSITE
DoItInPublic.com

TWITTER
Twitter.com/DoItInPublic

INSTAGRAM
Instagram.com/DoItInPublic

LINKEDIN
LinkedIn.com/in/DoItInPublic

Side Hustle, 9–5, Start-Up or Ready to Scale: Learn the Secret Weapon to Take Your Dream to the Next Level

Are you tired of your business not evolving into what you dreamed it could be? Or maybe you work full time, and that side hustle has not turned into a profitable business. Is the operation and management of your business bogging you down? Do you want to leave your 9–5? Or are you considering putting your business on the shelf and going back to work because you just can't gain traction?

Whether you want to start a business, have a side hustle and a 9–5 or are currently running a business at any level, there is more success available to you.

There is no time like the present for women to start and create a business. It doesn't have to be a dream any longer. There is more support and resources available to you now than ever before. Don't let the fear of failure or the fear of success prevent you from taking the next step. There is a need for more women-owned small- and medium-sized businesses now more than at any other time. Someone needs the dream that is in your heart to be fulfilled. You have the solution to someone's problem. You have a product or service that can make a difference in someone's life.

There's no reason why you should be stuck at the same level for years. If you want to start, grow or take your business to the next level, I know you'll find the interview with Lori Battle enlightening. −Conversation with Lisa C. Williams

Lisa Charlene Williams is the Founder of the #SmartHustle #SmartGrind movement (amiontheverge.com), an initiative to help female entrepreneurs succeed in business and life, stop working themselves to death and become the Doyennes of their industry, a woman who is the most respected or prominent person in a particular field.

Conversation with Lori Battle

Share about Coaching Designed by Lori and how you are helping and encouraging women to start and grow their businesses.

Lori Battle: I always use myself as the poster challenge, and I share my story with my client of how I started when I was twenty years old. I didn't have a business background. I didn't have a bunch of money in the bank. I didn't have any investors, but I did have a lot of confidence in myself. I knew a little bit of something, and I knew that was better than knowing a lot of nonsense. So, Coaching Design by Lori is basically my whole life experience as a young woman starting a business with nothing but a hundred dollars and how I grew that into a seven-figure business by the time I was in my mid-twenties. I teach women that there are a bunch of excuses that they can sit on, but there are a lot of open opportunities that they can take advantage of. Why don't they take advantage of opportunities that can get them moving and get them in a position to start their business? Or how about they grow it from just being out of their garage into an actual business forefront? That's what Coaching Design by Lori is. It's about helping women to launch, grow and connect their business ideas and dreams.

Perfect. What would you say are the advantages of starting a business for women who currently have a job?

Lori Battle: Oh, wow! I think it's absolutely a must because you should not be helping to build someone else's dream. You should be more concerned with how to build your legacy for your kids and your grandkids. You work for time, but you should also be carving out enough time to build your dreams, even if you're working full time. One of the advantages would eventually be more freedom.

What are the biggest myths out there when it comes to transitioning from a job to owning a business?

Lori Battle: People are persuaded into starting a business by companies that market to those dreamers, but they can be misleading. They often make people feel like they are going to have increased flexibility and better quality of life or that they will be able to take care of their kids. Ultimately, that is what you want your business to do, but the reality is that you are going to have to sacrifice—sacrifice your time by missing important events sometimes and sacrifice your comfort. If you really want to make your business generate revenue, then you are going to have to put in some elbow grease. It's going to take thinking outside of the box. It's going to take being available to attend classes to learn about your trade or whatever your field is. You have to be knowledgeable about what you're doing, so I encourage you to be able to go to classes or take some kind of seminar. That's the investment part.

Building a dream is going to take investing into that dream. Maybe you have discretionary income that you would normally spend on extra shoes, purses, treats, or a girls' weekend trip. As a business owner, you are going to have to decide: *Where do I allocate this money? Do I put this into a marketing plan or do I put this into the weekend trip with the girls?* There is going to be some sacrifice, at least early on.

What would you say are some common misconceptions women have about hiring a coach to help them start or grow their business?

Lori Battle: Some of the things women tend to have misconceptions about when hiring a coach are affordability and effectiveness. They don't believe that they can afford a coach. Another would be the myth that coaches don't really help you grow your business. Women especially are concerned with what the investment will be and if they can afford it. They wonder if they invest in a coach if the coach will really help them get to where they need to be. Trusting is definitely a key factor. The third thing women struggle with is being honest about what they really need and how a coach can help them because, sometimes, you run into people who claim they know it all and don't feel like they need a coach.

What are some of the most common fears that you've heard women specifically express about starting their own business?

Lori Battle: The first and biggest is the fear of competition. Women tend to worry about what everyone else is doing. *Are they doing it better? Will I be able to compete with them? Am I qualified enough to be able to compete?* So, competition is truly one of the biggest fears I see. I help my clients focus on their lane, on who they are, and on what they have to offer.

Women especially can also be concerned with: *What if I am successful at this? What if this really does work? What if I do blow up? What if I do make ten million dollars?* Not knowing what is on the other side of their idea or concept is very fearful for some people, so they would rather settle for safe, and they would rather settle for what they do know versus the unknown. Lastly, I see the fear of rejection: *Will anybody like it? Will people buy it?*

How can you help them get past those three fears?

Lori Battle: I can help women get past those three fears by helping them to understand the value they possess and by helping them understand that it takes confidence to succeed. If you are not confident in what you are doing, then you are devaluing yourself. I show women how to be confident. Those are two concepts that I work on because, once upon a time, I was not as confident as I am now, but when I learned how to be confident in my value, that's when my business took off.

While women business owners are the fastest growing segment of entrepreneurs, what perceived obstacles do you see that might be discouraging some women from going into business?

Lori Battle: Being in business for over twenty years now, I don't see women not pursuing their business dreams. I find that women are seeing this time as an open field and seeing now as their time and they are seizing the moment. I don't see the reluctance we saw twenty years ago. I see the polar opposite.

But as we discussed before, obstacles I can help women who work with me get over are, getting past fear by showing them what it takes to start growing and have a successful business. My tagline is, "I help women who want to either go into business or grow into business." I help women learn the plethora of other aspects of business that one needs to know and be prepared for along the way.

What are a couple of pitfalls that you see women make when they first start their business?

Lori Battle: I see women being too eager and not taking the necessary precautions to keep themselves from losing money as well as not knowing how to say no. As business owners, we need to realize that every opportunity presented to us is not for us. Everybody who is extending a hand to help us is not really trying to help us.

So, women especially have to be careful that they don't fall prey to people, thinking that people who validate what they are doing always have their best interest in mind.

What I always tell prospects and clients is to remember that their dream started with them. Their idea started with them. It's going to be up to them as to where they take it, so they can't come in and expect anybody to fill their shoes. You've got to get fortified. You've got to build your resistance to failure. You've got to decide that failure is not an option. You must build your resilience muscle to be successful in business.

What inspired you to become a coach for women entrepreneurs?

Lori Battle: When I started to see a lot of women around me who were brilliant and who had great ideas struggling to build their business and put the pieces of the puzzle together, it pulled on my heartstrings. I have a heart to help people. That's my nature. I enjoy offering advice, so I just did what comes naturally to me. I have achieved a level of success. I made seven figures in my twenties. Building and growing a business, I can do in my sleep, so wanting to help other people and women was just a natural thing for me.

I also wanted to help shorten the time for women that it can take to build a successful business. My desire came from a natural place to be able to help. I got into coaching because I really wanted to solve a problem for women.

Can you share a lesson you learned early on that still affects how you do business today?

Lori Battle: I must practice what I preach, so I had to learn how to put on my own artillery and become a soldier. I was looking for people to come rescue me, to come help me, and to come do the things that only I could do to fulfill my dream because God gave the dream to me. I stopped expecting others and my family to make my dream come to fruition. The life lesson for me was to learn what business artillery is (which is the willingness to do what I needed to do, the willingness to find the resources and support I needed) and stop expecting people to rescue me and hoping that I would just become successful and become a soldier in my business.

What are the most important questions women should ask themselves if they are thinking of starting a business?

Lori Battle: *Do I have the time? Do I have the resources? Am I willing to invest my own finances in my dream?*

What questions should they ask when they are seeking a coach?

Lori Battle: When hiring a coach, you should ask: "What is your proven track record?" "How can I find out information about you—either social media or a website, anything published about you?" Then third, "What can you tell me is your best success out of all your coaching clients?"

Can you share a success story of a woman you helped?

Lori Battle: One of my best success stories is that I have a young lady who came to my event for the first year, and she did not even have a business idea. When she left my event, she not only started her event two weeks later, but she also began coaching with me about three months after the event. Now, fast forward three years later, she has a franchise of businesses around the country. After attending my Dream conference and receiving inspiration and education, she went from not having a business to doing what was necessary to start her business. She saw the value in hiring me as a coach, which fast-tracked her success, and the dream and vision she had inside was unleashed. She's one of my best biggest successes, and we've been working together ever since.

What would you leave women with who are thinking about starting a business or who have started a business and are struggling?

Lori Battle: I would say go for it. I would say don't over think it. Don't think yourself out of it. If you feel passionate about your business idea, then go for it. There's no better time than right now. It doesn't matter if the economy is good or bad; it's always a good time to start a business.

About Lori Battle

Over the past 20 years, Lori Battle has inspired thousands of men and women to dream big and live their dream life. She is a Motivational Speaker, Event Producer, Entrepreneur, award-winning Success Coach and Philanthropist. Her journey as an entrepreneur began at the age of 20, and she started her first business while still a college student at U.C.L.A. with just a hundred-dollar investment. By the time she was in her mid-20s, she owned multiple successful businesses that generated seven figures annually. As a sought-after keynote speaker and expert entrepreneur panelist, she has been invited to speak at Universities, large women's conferences, churches, and private events across the country.

Most recently, she appeared as a featured guest on Black Hollywood Live and Behind the scenes radio show, which has over 6 million listeners worldwide. As a Success Coach, her clients include business professionals, entrepreneurs, and celebrities. In 2013, she launched the highly successful dream girl luncheon, a motivational networking event for women. In 2016, she formed her non-profit charity called The Dream Girl Foundation, which helps young women from underserved communities with entrepreneurial training, self-care education, and scholarships to college. 2018 will be her best year yet, as she takes her dream big tour to 12 cities nationwide, inspiring one million men and women to press play on their dreams!

WEBSITE
LoriBattle.com

FACEBOOK
Facebook.com/YourBestLiving

INSTAGRAM
Instagram.com/LoriBattle

How to Attract the Right Candidates and Reduce Employee Turnover Through Recruitment Marketing

Is your company ensuring that top talent desires to work with you? Is your HR department handling the messaging that is being distributed via social media about your workplace culture? Are you aware of the importance placed on recruitment marketing in today's landscape of workplace diversity, women's leadership, #metoo initiatives, and more?

As the founder and president of Strategic & Creative Marketing Inc. (SC Marketing), Susan MacNicol's expertise in the field of recruitment marketing comes from over 25 years of working at major corporations and Fortune 500 companies in both the marketing division and in the recruiting division. MacNicol has background and knowledge from those areas that she combines into strategies for employment branding and recruitment marketing to help companies better attract and retain employees.

It is critical today to ensure that your company's messaging is clear and accurately communicates your company culture to attract top talent that complements the corporate culture. Unfortunately, your HR department does not have this type of marketing expertise and their time is focused on the basics of posting jobs, interviewing candidates, and hiring new employees.

Susan MacNicol is a forerunner in the corporate and recruitment marketing space. In addition to 25 years in corporate marketing at companies across the U.S. and in Europe, Susan also served as a recruiter at Johnson and Johnson, Sears Corporation, and DeVry Education Group (now Adtalem Global Education) where she hired over 400 professors nationwide for DeVry and more than 150 sales professionals and managers for Johnson and Johnson companies in the pharmaceutical division. Plus, she delivered innovative recruitment marketing strategies in consulting roles for Sears Corporate and OfficeMax Corporate.

If you have primarily focused on spending your budget on only traditional HR processes and you've tasked your marketing department to focus on messaging and strategies to sell your products or services, it's time for you to merge these two areas. Consider hiring a specialist that unites marketing expertise and recruiting knowledge to create a compelling Employment Brand and develop the Recruitment Marketing tactics that reach and attract sought-after talent.

By developing this often-underutilized strategy, your company stands out! Only 28% of companies have made Employer Branding a priority. While job seekers research companies and vet opportunities, they'll have a realistic view of your organization, your culture, and the reasons why they should join your team. And, if candidates fully understand your culture, there's an increased probability that they'll fit the culture right from the start and remain with your company longer after they're hired. Do you currently have a recruitment marketing plan in place to attract the best talent to join your organization? With the current and disruptive business landscape, it's critical to address gender policies, protection, and opportunities for women in the workplace, along with diversity initiatives.

If you have policies in place, then communicate them through recruitment marketing initiatives. Highlight your responsive and supportive corporate culture to encourage candidates to learn more about your organization and to also retain talent within the company. Take a few moments and learn about why you need to incorporate employment branding and recruitment marketing into your current marketing strategy. I know you'll find the interview with Susan MacNicol enlightening. −Conversation with Lisa C. Williams

Lisa Charlene Williams is the Founder of the #SmartHustle #SmartGrind movement (amiontheverge.com), an initiative to help female entrepreneurs succeed in business and life, stop working themselves to death and become the Doyennes of their industry, a woman who is the most respected or prominent person in a particular field.

Conversation with Susan MacNicol

Share about SC Marketing Inc. and how you help medium-size and large companies and corporations.

Susan MacNicol: SC Marketing is focused on helping organizations craft and identify their employment brand, as well as communicate that brand to the exact target audience they need to reach, which in turn will attract the top talent and fill the open roles in the company more effectively and quickly.

What is recruitment marketing?

Susan MacNicol: Recruitment marketing incorporates all the aspects of marketing, everything from planning, branding, and strategy. However, recruitment marketing is geared towards attracting talent as opposed to promoting a product or service.

Describe at least one big problem you specialize in solving with regard to recruitment marketing.

Susan MacNicol: Organizations sometimes struggle with how to promote their organizational culture and their current employment opportunities. We work with organizations to create a cohesive strategy that will establish the employer's brand and clarify what it represents. We call this the EVP, which stands for 'Employee Value Proposition.' Once we have established the organization's EVP, we then execute a strategy to communicate it to the public and the right talent target.

Describe the outcome that can be achieved by working with you.

Susan MacNicol: As a result of working with SC Marketing, organizations can expect to achieve a very clear, positive and accurate message about their culture. This resonates with potential candidates and new employees and decreases employee turnover. Due to the fact that we have effectively communicated the organization's culture and provided a glimpse of the experience candidates can expect, the culture fit is more likely to occur, and new employee will then often thrive at the organization.

What are the advantages to companies hiring employees that share their company culture?

Susan MacNicol: First, I want to share a statistic. Did you know that 83 percent of the turnover is attributed to a clash in company culture? This happens because companies often only look at skills and educational background. The key to decreasing turnover would be to ensure candidates understand the company's culture. For example, if the company's culture is very aggressive and competitive, then you want people who will survive and thrive in that type of environment. You don't want someone who is more docile and collaborative. That personality wouldn't succeed. They may appear to be the right fit on paper, but you will have a lot of unhappy people; that results in a frequent turnover and ultimately impacts productivity. There's tons of research showing that when an organization has highly engaged employees, they are able to achieve the highest profitability. So, having the right people in the right culture, and a highly-engaged staff, helps an organization's profitably and innovation.

What do you feel are the biggest myths out there when it comes to the way companies have hired in the past compared to how they should be looking at hiring now?

Susan MacNicol: In the past when the job market was flooded with applicants, companies very often had a self-centered attitude with respect to their hiring process. Their outlook was:

- If an applicant wants to work for us, they'll go through this long application. They will deal with whatever we throw at them.
- They don't need to know all the advantages of working at our organization.
- What can the applicant do for our organization?

However, there has been a shift in many companies' views because, now, more and more, it has become a buyer's market or a candidate's market. There is a lower unemployment rate and more available opportunities, with many highly-skilled roles going unfilled for months and even more than a year. Job seekers have an upper hand and are now researching 8–12 resources—from websites, social media, Glassdoor and career pages—before they even apply for a job. They are asking more questions about career opportunity, cultural fit, and the organization's mission, vision, and business goals. They want to know the company's views on issues such as work-life balance and community involvement. The power has shifted, and companies need to impress and entice many top performers to join their organizations.

What are some common misconceptions about hiring an outside consultant or agency when they have an in-house HR department that handles hiring?

Susan MacNicol: The misconceptions center around the capabilities of their internal staff. Recruitment and marketing are very specialized areas, and organizations' internal staff must have the marketing skills as well as a knowledge of recruiting. It's rare to find this combination of knowledge in both areas. Most HR professionals are focused on their roles and responsibilities in the HR function; they are not marketers, and they don't have the skill set that is commonly found in marketing professionals. An outside consulting company that specializes in, and fully understands, both the marketing and recruiting functions within a company is invaluable in pulling both teams together and delivering an effective program across these two distinct operating areas.

What are some of the most common fears companies are facing today as they are looking to hire new employees?

Susan MacNicol: Some of the challenges and fears from a company perspective is that the hiring will take a long time, and often the new hire is not a good fit and only remains with the company for a short time. This impacts productivity and affects overall sales and profits. By having a role open for a long time, and shifting more work to the remaining employees, it can also have a negative impact on employee satisfaction and increase turnover in the department. Recruiters work with hiring managers from each division, and these managers need to fill roles quickly to complete the business goals for their team, so they often put a lot of pressure on the recruiting team to fill the role quickly. However, specialized or hard-to-fill roles can remain open for 300 days, 450 days, so we're talking over a year, and still not be filled. This is where building the talent pools, communicating with past applicants in the HR databases, using a strong employment brand, and recruitment marketing tactics make the difference.

How can they get past these fears?

Susan MacNicol: The best way to overcome these challenges is to have an expert focused on how their organization and company culture are perceived, what is their employment brand, what does it represent, and then, how is it communicated. The organization must be transparent, very realistic, available and accessible to applicants who want to learn more. Organizations must also nurture other leads they have obtained from potential past candidates or applicants who expressed some interest in the company. If they are nurturing and keeping in touch with those applicants, then they are building and maintaining a talent pool that can be quickly tapped into, and candidates can be found, interviewed and hired more rapidly and moved to the interview and hiring stage.

What other perceived obstacles do you see that might be preventing companies and corporations from seeking the help of an outside recruitment marketing professional?

Susan MacNicol: Often companies will attempt to rely on their in-house marketing team instead of hiring or consulting with an outside recruitment marketing professional. However, their in-house marketing team's goals, their bonuses, everything

EXPERT PROFILES · 65

they do is not focused on helping the recruiting team. Their entire focus is on increasing sales of the product or service and raising consumer or business awareness of the core product or service of the company. So, they do not have the recruiting expertise, they are not available to focus on recruiting needs, and they don't have the time or expertise to develop and launch recruitment marketing strategies that will work well with the recruiting team's efforts, goals, and technologies.

Can you share an example of how you have helped a corporation with recruitment marketing, and how did it help them overcome an obstacle and achieve a successful outcome?

Susan MacNicol: Email Campaign and Interdepartmental Strategy – I recently worked for a global education organization and created an internal partnership between the recruiting team and the sales/development team in order to recruit highly-skilled, hard-to-find Nurse Educator Professors. In the past, the recruiting team created job fairs at the local campuses to recruit these professionals and spent budgets on emails, direct mail, and ads to promote the event. However, the final results were generally under 15 attendees at the event, with only one to three hires. Instead, I worked with the sales/development team, which already had relationships in place at local hospitals and medical centers and interacted weekly with the same professionals we were trying to recruit. So, together we created an email campaign to reach these individuals with the details about the career opportunity. Within two weeks, we had 13 applicants and hired ten new Nurse Educator Professors at no cost to the company!

A Small Marketing Tactic to Increase Candidate Flow – A few years ago, I worked with a retail corporation as they embarked on opening 12 new stores in ten different markets. I was tasked with making sure we had a good flow of candidates for the job fairs to ensure the fair would run smoothly and we could rapidly hire the talent needed to open the new stores. The candidate flow was traditionally low, and the recruitment marketing budget was virtually non-existent. So, I recommended one simple marketing tactic that completely flipped the switch to promote the job fairs to the local market and deliver a better pool of applicants. I created what is known as Outdoor Bandit Signs, which are small signs with little metal legs that are placed in the grass, like the signs used to advertise real estate or an open house. So, we created these signs for each local market to promote the Job Fair, including the date and time. Each store was located on a major street, so we placed the signs in the grass on the outskirts to attract the eyes of potential applicants. This simple change increased the applicant flow by about 35 percent.

Susan, what inspired you to get certified as a Recruitment Marketing Specialist, and what value do you bring to a corporation having that certification?

Susan MacNicol: It's kind of a funny story that my very first job out of college was working as a copywriter for a recruitment marketing company in Chicago. Also, one of my college internships was in recruitment marketing. So, I have really come full circle after 25 years of experience and an MBA. I am now back in the recruitment marketing arena and with a lot more knowledge and experience. The certification enabled me to complete courses to ensure that I had the latest knowledge and techniques in my 'toolbox' to assist companies in developing the recruitment marketing that is effective.

Can you share a lesson you learned early on that still impacts how you do business today?

Susan MacNicol: I was a marketing intern with a financial company when I was 19 years old and didn't really know much about business. I was tasked with checking into some information for an upcoming trade show. Well, I placed a call, but no one answered, so I left a message. Because I only left a message and did not follow up, I didn't get the information. The person I was working for was very firm about it and said, "Listen, if you need information, you have to be on top of it. You have to close all the loops on the things you're doing. You have to follow up and be professional in everything you do. You can't just come to a meeting and say, 'Yeah, they never called me back, so I don't have the information.'" Since then, I've always been on top of details and 'buttoned up' on each aspect of work that I am tasked with to make sure the entire project is flawless. I learned the lesson to be thorough and pay attention to every detail at a young age, and it has enabled me to succeed throughout my entire career.

What's the most important question corporations should ask themselves as they consider hiring new employees and going about it in the traditional manner that they have in the past?

Susan MacNicol: They have to reexamine the entire process and take a realistic look at the current talent marketplace. The availability of talent and how they attract talent—that's really a new game in the world.

So, the questions they should ask are:

- How are we positioned for attracting talent?
- How can we do a better job of communicating what it's really like to work as part of our team and part of our company?
- How can we attract the top talent that will be the best fit in our culture?
- How do we find, reach, and then attract the talent we want to come to our company?
- What are candidates saying about us—what are they reading and hearing about our company and our culture?
- What are current staff members saying about our company, and how can we share the positive feedback from happy employees with the public?
- How can we maintain ongoing communication with past applicants, provide compelling content regularly and connect with them for upcoming career opportunities?

What's the most important consideration corporations should think about when evaluating whether to go with their in-house HR department or hire an outside consultant?

Susan MacNicol: Corporations must evaluate the talent they currently have in their HR department and try to identify if they already have someone who has a strong marketing background. If they are unable to identify someone already within their team, they should consider bringing in a consultant with both recruiting and marketing expertise. It is in their best interest to have a marketing person creating the marketing strategy and plans who also has the knowledge of HR and recruiting.

What would you like to leave corporations with, and what is the benefit they will receive working with you?

Susan MacNicol: Realize the impact on your entire organization when you have roles that are open for a long amount of time, and you can't find the right talent to move your company forward. It impacts the overall organization, the profitability, but it also affects morale when individuals are doing double work and positions are left unfilled. The most profitable companies have the best culture and hire exceptional talent. So, if there's any doubt or question about spending money on employment branding and recruitment marketing, I implore you to look at the dollars you're losing by having unfilled roles or a revolving door of poor hires. This should inspire you to consider hiring someone skilled at recruiting and marketing, who can effectively develop the Employee Brand and communicate it through effective Recruitment Marketing to attract the candidates that will fit the organization and enable the company to grow.

About Susan MacNicol

Susan MacNicol has more than 25 years of business experience spanning several industries, including media, entertainment, retail, higher education, and data. Her roles have ranged from marketing, employment branding, and client relations to sales, recruiting, and training. Past management roles were at STARZ Encore Group, Orbit Satellite and Radio Networks (Rome, Italy), Samuel Goldwyn Studios, Columbia TriStar Television Distribution and Columbia Pictures (Sony Pictures Entertainment).

Susan established her marketing consulting firm, Strategic & Creative Marketing Inc., in 2001 and has completed projects for non-profits, small businesses, and major global companies such as Experian, Nielsen, Charter Business, Office Max, Sears, and Ericsson. Projects include strategic marketing, branding, recruitment marketing, creative tactics, training, promotion and publicity campaigns, advertising and sales campaigns.

Her educational background includes an MBA from Pepperdine University and a BA in Marketing Communications from Columbia College, Chicago. Susan lives with her husband and two sons in the Chicago suburbs and enjoys travel, biking, hiking, and supporting local community groups focused on improving education for children and providing opportunities for women.

WEBSITE

SCMarketingInc.com

FACEBOOK

Facebook.com/SCMarketingInc

TWITTER

Twitter.com/SusanMacNicol

LINKEDIN

LinkedIn.com/company/Strategic-&-Creative-Marketing-Inc.

Through Community and Collaboration with Others, It Is Possible for Women to Live the Life of Their Dreams

Are you living your life according to the model that society has approved for women? You graduate from college, land a well-paying job in corporate America, and then get married and have kids after investing a few years in your career. But what if you're not truly happy in your career? Instead of sticking with a model that others have designed, why not take a leap of faith and create your own model for living? That's exactly what a new generation of women are seeking to do—revolutionize the society-approved model of how women should live and work.

Many women feel unfulfilled in their current occupation. If you are one of the women who believe you have a deeper purpose for living and a higher calling to fulfill, then it's time for you to design the life that you want to live. By doing so, you will be able to better impact the world with your unique gift and talent.

Entrepreneurship is one of the best ways to design the life that you want to live. It will help you to evolve fully into the woman you were put here to be as well as get an in-depth look at what your purpose is. Do you want to discover what pathways of opportunity are created through entrepreneurship? Do you want to help bridge the gap between business, womanhood, and sisterhood? If you want more information on this, I know you'll find Meagan Ward's interview helpful. —Conversation with Lisa C. Williams

Lisa Charlene Williams is the Founder of the #SmartHustle #SmartGrind movement (amiontheverge.com), an initiative to help female entrepreneurs succeed in business and life, stop working themselves to death and become the Doyennes of their industry, a woman who is the most respected or prominent person in a particular field.

Conversation with Meagan Ward

What is "The Powerful Women Initiative," and how are you helping women?

Meagan Ward: *The Powerful Women Initiative* is a culture of excellence for women of color. It stems from a personal narrative—my being a woman of excellence, graduating from college, and being on a rigorous rhyme in executing my goals, but also needing a sense of community. Women like me are often on the go, and we don't always have time to socialize. So, I decided to create an organization where women can find out what they are going through, whether it's personal or professional. It also serves as a level of accountability for living our ultimate dream as well as provides a way for us to help one another in reaching the goals to accomplish our dreams.

What are the advantages of a community, like the one you are fostering, with "The Powerful Women Initiative"?

Meagan Ward: The number one advantage is accountability. I remember when I started *Power of a Woman*, a woman named Brittni Brown helped me with it. She provided her expertise. I had my expertise, and we were able to collaborate. We held each other accountable, and we bonded over what we were great at. We could execute our goals together. I think that's what women are starting to understand, that we don't have to do it alone anymore.

The woman who is trying to climb the corporate ladder or who is trying to get to the CEO level can better do so with the help of other women. The woman who is building her business and trying to leave her nine-to-five will be encouraged to find that there is a whole community of women who are trying to do the same thing. We can share our challenges, as well as our wins, to inspire each other and strategize on new ways that we can help one another level up.

Collaboration remains a very new concept for women who are aggressively pursuing their goals. But with collaboration, I always like to say, we can thrive together. When *The Powerful Women Initiative* first launched in 2014, we had hundreds of women come to the launching. From this first launch, we now have women building businesses together. We have women promoting one another's services. We have women chatting over coffee and tea, exchanging valuable information which helps them along the next journey in their life. We also have women providing mentorship due to collaboration.

For me, I know a major turning point came when I brought on an international client who I met through Instagram and different women empowerment events. Her mentorship changed my life because it not only leveled up my business, but I was also able to see how she did business. I saw how she took her product line from her kitchen to Sally Beauty stores all over the world. By being connected with her, I was inspired to collaborate with other women. Collaboration creates a domino effect among women. When one woman collaborates and is connected, she is going to collaborate with another woman, which often results in a domino effect taking place.

What are some of the myths out there regarding joining a group or attending a women's conference or event?

Meagan Ward: One myth that I deal with daily is that powerful women all can't be at the top. I'm from Detroit, an urban city which has a large group of enterprising women who accumulate in their respective lanes. So, Detroit has women who are leading in their field but who are also sharing a sisterhood together. In that sisterhood, they are helping one another rise to the top. These Detroit women include Melissa Butler, one of the most successful women entrepreneurs in the beauty industry who went from a 'Shark Tank' rejection to having her products sold in Target. There's also Brittni Brown, who is one of the top African American publicists in the United States. There are many women who are killing it in their respective fields but who are also sharing in the sisterhood, which is very important. We are leaders in our communities, and we are making a change together. The most important thing about women empowerment is that we can all rise together, and we can all win together.

That is excellent. What would you say some common misconceptions are when women get together in a group like "The Powerful Women Initiative"?

Meagan Ward: One is that you can't mix business with friendship. I think what society needs to understand is that women don't work in that way. A lot of times we are bonding over womanhood, and within womanhood comes the ability to be nurtured, the ability to be a businesswoman, and the ability to be friends. A lot of the clients I've been in business with have become my friends. So, that is one myth that I am working to change with my initiative.

What are some of the fears women experience as they are on the road to pursuing their dreams, visions, and plans for their business?

Meagan Ward: Recently, I became a speaker for the U.S. Embassy on women empowerment. I was invited overseas to give a glimpse of women empowerment in a second world country. Even though we live and work in different parts of the world, at the end of the day, we have a common goal. So, one of my main purposes when I traveled to this country was to see what that common goal was. By talking to women in the U.S. and having experiences with women while traveling, I was able to see that we all want to be fulfilled, but to be fulfilled, we must change our mindset from learned behavior. Society has shaped how women should live their lives from being a businesswoman, a wife, a mother, and essentially a woman. If we want to live unapologetically, we must rethink the behavior we have learned. For me, after I graduated from college, I was unfulfilled in my job position. I knew in my heart that it wasn't for me. The scariest thing I've ever done was to leave my job because that was the model I had known all my life.

One of the ways for women to get past their fears and live the life they want is for them to go on a self-discovery journey. They need to understand that they are here on earth for a reason, and their job is to figure out why they are here. It is key for them to learn about themselves, learn about what they like, what they don't like, what kills them, what doesn't kill them, what their gifts and what their talents are, and ultimately how those gifts and talents can help others.

By getting clarity, you become confident, and confidence is what eliminates fears.

What are the pitfalls or common mistakes that you see women make in their business when they are not connected?

Meagan Ward: First, let me say that I believe in the power of community because I believe in the power of change. People make things happen. The woman who made it on a Forbes list or the woman who got her product in a thousand Target stores, that happened because of a relationship that was built. When we open ourselves up to a community, not only do we open ourselves up to information, but we also open ourselves up to developing a relationship that can change our lives. Many women ask me: "What's the blueprint to get to where I want to be?" I always tell them that the key is relationship building. Nothing is more powerful than a relationship—not a book, not a strategy, not anything. So, I always advocate for building relationships, not only for business but for enhancing your life.

Due to the recent rise of the self-care movement, women are getting smarter about how we take care of ourselves mentally, emotionally and spiritually. That care, however, also comes in relationship building. Connecting with other women can help elevate us in those three ways as well. In the last couple of years, I've focused on that because I know to reach the level of success I want to reach, I need to be stronger emotionally, mentally and spiritually, so I'm surrounding myself with women who can help elevate me in all those areas.

Can you share an example of a woman you worked with and what you were able to help her achieve?

Meagan Ward: Brittni Brown is a client story of mine that is great to share. I worked with her, strategizing on her business for about a year, and then did her brand development. I helped her change from helping fashion shows and beauty brands to targeting start-up entrepreneurs with a purpose and helping them tell their stories to the media. She was able to move into entrepreneurship full-time with her business, and she now has one of the most successful public relations firms in Detroit. It's amazing to see her and her growth and how she changed her mindset about how she lived her life.

At the end of the day, even though I do branding and women empowerment, I want to see women live the life of their dreams and for them to know that it is possible to do so.

What inspired you to become a leader for women and for African American businesswomen?

Meagan Ward: To be honest, I was raised by a single mom. She was the first person in our family to go to college. She built an investment company with my grandfather, and they named it after me. So, I remember being six years old and knowing there was a company called MEG Investments. At that early age, I was still learning the concept of business, but I was so amused and inspired that my grandfather and mom named their business after me. Ever since then, I knew I wanted to be a businesswoman. I didn't know what kind of businesswoman, but from seeing my family create businesses and have ideas, I was certainly inspired. Of course, my mom was my first mentor. One of her values is always being kind to other women. She was always complimenting other women. When we saw them in the mall, she would say how beautiful they looked, or she would invite her co-workers over for brunches at her house, and that type of action is what prompted me to be an activist for women empowerment.

Can you share a lesson that you learned early on that still impacts how you do business today?

Meagan Ward: It's great to provide an amazing customer service experience, but understanding what the service can do for someone is equally important. For example, I do branding. I help women brand their businesses so that they can live their dream life. Understanding that I do more than just own a business, I know that I also help shape the mindsets of women and help change their journey in doing that which is more comfortable for them.

What's the lesson that you learned earlier on that applies to the example you just gave?

Meagan Ward: The lesson is that services go deeper. What we're offering as a business owner goes deeper than that first level. It's not just a service or a product, but it's enhancing the person, whether through inspiration, mentorship, or accountability. When I take on a client, I take a whole lot of pride in what I'm doing because it's not just me providing a service; it's me helping them to shape their life to leave a legacy.

When I first started, I often thought, *Oh, I taught myself how to design, and I can help women do branding and marketing.* Now, I think, *Wow, these women are really living their dream lives.* I'm speechless every day because when I inquire as to how former clients are doing, the response is often along the lines of "Oh, this client left her job" or "This client just opened up a salon" or "This client just got featured in 'Beauty' magazine." So, yes, it's more than just a service.

What are the most important questions women entrepreneurs should ask themselves if they are starting a business?

Meagan Ward: One thing they should ask themselves is: *Is it purposeful for my life, and can it create a profit?* The reason why I say so is that we are in this winning season of women, but we don't talk about our lapses. We don't talk about things that we are not doing. There are more women creating businesses, and there are a lot of women who are making money, but that is something that is not talked about whatsoever. So, part of what I do when I'm strategizing with a client is to make sure that their business is purposeful and that it has a demand that can create a profit.

What should female business owners consider when evaluating how they should invest in their business to level up their brand?

Meagan Ward: From the perspective of a start-up entrepreneur, I think it's important for us to understand return on investment. For example, if I am investing in an event or a conference, and I want to go to this conference, what benefit am I going to get from it? If it is a three-hundred-dollar conference, am I learning about sales? What are the key benefits of it?

What would you say to a woman who might attend one of "The Powerful Women Initiative" events? What is the experience she will have, and what will she walk away with?

Meagan Ward: Our events are one of a kind. We focus on all five senses when you walk in a room, from the programming to the speakers to the interviews. I've been to so many different events, but *The Powerful Women Initiative* event is truly unique because we focus on womanhood as a whole. Then we also focus on a woman's experience in personal development, business, and sisterhood. We also provide a curated experience that is perfect for each of those stages.

Women who attend *The Powerful Women Initiative* event can expect to elevate themselves by learning from other women. They will learn self-care practices on how to take care of themselves. They will learn how not to burn out. They will learn how to overcome their fears. They will learn how to level up in their business and not operate it at a mediocre level. They will also have the chance to create relationships that will enhance their life.

If it wasn't for the stand I have for women, I wouldn't be where I am today. At *The Powerful Women Initiative* event, you have women who are just getting started in their purpose journey as well as women who have been on their purpose journey for ten years. The exchange between the two is the value that comes from *The Powerful Women Initiative* event.

About Meagan Ward

Powerfully poised in entrepreneurial activism and global empowerment, Meagan Ward is the incomparable impact leader, strategist and branding maven consistently positioning women for greatness in business and life. Meagan's keen expertise as an industry trailblazer has propelled hundreds of women forward through the transformation of passion into purpose, helping each woman to uniquely define and create success on their own terms—something she achieved for herself in just three years.

Meagan has created an enterprising network of women as owner of Creatively Flawless, a branding agency for women-owned businesses; owner of FEMOLOGY, Detroit's first female-focused co-working space; and creator of The Powerful Women, the acclaimed movement highlighting powerful women in Detroit which cultivates rich experiences for women to embrace, learn, bond, and uplift through sisterhood. Meagan's vocal advocacy for women integration and progress has led her to become an appointed speaker for the U.S. Embassy. Upon earning this permanent position in 2017,

Meagan was immediately called to share perspective on global scale women empowerment in Tbilisi, Georgia.

Meagan has received notable honors, including the 2018 Career Mastered Trailblazer Award, Detroit Young Professionals Vanguard Award, *Essence* Magazine's "Young Phenom," *Crain's* 20 in their 20's 2018, City of Detroit's Testimonial Resolution Honor, Walker's Legacy Power 25, State of Michigan Special Tribute, HOUR Detroit's "She Means Business" feature, and Western Michigan University's College of Business Young Alumni of the Year Award.

Meagan has been featured in *Black Enterprise*, *The Huffington Post*, *Crain's*, *Rolling Out*, and a host of other media outlets. Her dedicated brand work has been displayed in Times Square, Target, *Vogue*, *Essence* magazine, and more.

WEBSITE
CreativelyFlawless.com

INSTAGRAM
Instagram.com/MeaganVoguist

LINKEDIN
LinkedIn.com/in/Meagan-Ward-75a06760/

Navigating the Journey to the Top of Your Industry Shouldn't Be Done Alone – Journey with Me and Other Mogulistas

Are you struggling to start, grow, or scale your business? Do you sometimes wonder whether you should throw in the towel and go back to work? Are you good at envisioning the big picture, but the day-to-day details make you want to jump back in bed? You most likely have a great business or an important vision, but you just need help executing, or maybe your life is swallowing you up, and you need some coaching support to get your momentum going.

There are many aspects that make you feel whole as a businesswoman, and it's not just about business. Maintaining a healthy lifestyle, eating habits and a balance of your time are all important areas, especially for a woman. Maybe you're not feeling confident or respected as an expert. Indeed, there are a host of challenges that we as women face when we're embarking on the journey to better ourselves, our businesses, and our brand.

You don't have to journey alone. Many women who are building their business are experiencing the same challenges that you've encountered. It can feel very lonely going through challenges such as sickness or divorce, especially if you're also trying to build a business or brand. What you need is a coach and a community who will be transparent about their successes and failures. If you are stuck trying to get your business off the ground or are perplexed at trying to find purpose in your passion or passion in your purpose and need help in creating the ultimate roadmap for building your business, brand, and your life behind the scenes, I know you'll find the interview with Kynia Starkey enlightening.
−Conversation with Lisa C. Williams

Lisa Charlene Williams is the Founder of the #SmartHustle #SmartGrind movement (amiontheverge.com), an initiative to help female entrepreneurs succeed in business and life, stop working themselves to death and become the Doyennes of their industry, a woman who is the most respected or prominent person in a particular field.

Conversation with Kynia Starkey

What is a Mogulista? Share about the Fem Moguls Movement and how you are helping women make moves and journey to the top.

Kynia Starkey: A Mogulista is a woman who desires to be massively successful and who is willing to make moves to achieve that success and reach the top in their respective industries. It's a woman who wants to stand out and really hit the ground running with their purpose and their passion. The root of the word is mogul. So, it's really about a woman becoming financially secure and extremely savvy from a business perspective.

I was inspired to create Fem Moguls and the Mogulista movement to provide a community and offer my years of experience and support to help women navigate the many twists, turns, and potholes along the path to establishing, growing and scaling their business.

I am determined to help women streamline their journey to the top and help them achieve a balanced business and balanced life, or as I like to call it, the 'behind the scenes.' I assist in accomplishing this by helping them to concentrate and consolidate the effort they're putting into building their business and brand.

As a result, I help ease and relieve some of the stress that women carry on their journey. I strive to make it a more embraceable and enjoyable journey so that there isn't the feeling of simply hustling or grinding and not moving forward. One of the challenges we as women often face is that many of us lack the confidence we should have. I want women to feel like there's momentum behind the moves that they're making.

What are the advantages of working with you to help navigate the journey that a female business owner experiences?

Kynia Starkey: First and foremost, I like to provide women with practical tools and techniques to help guide their journey and give them a competitive edge without the actual struggles of competing. These tools include creating a plan for moving forward. Many of our journeys can be difficult to navigate because there is no detailed plan to use as a frame of reference for moving forward. I also encourage community and focus on creating an atmosphere of camaraderie, which is another inherent benefit. As women, it often seems as if we are always in a very competitive space, but in reality, we enjoy community and companionship. This movement is one way to help women come together through community, collaboration and with the confidence they need to achieve success.

What do you feel are the biggest myths that women believe about the journey of establishing, growing and scaling their business?

Kynia Starkey: I think many feel that they have to journey to the top alone, that there's no one else experiencing the same challenges that they've encountered. It can feel very lonely going through challenges such as illness or divorce. But those types of challenges, especially when also trying to build a business or brand, really underscore the importance of a coach and community. Many women also believe they have to sacrifice much of what exists behind the scenes in order to be successful, but again, a plan and a community help to facilitate navigating a balanced journey. So, the myth is not true; they aren't the only ones—there are challenges that are common to female entrepreneurs. They don't have to do it alone, and they can successfully navigate without having to sacrifice so much behind the scenes. I help them with feeling comfortable through my own transparency, which encourages them to do the same and share. This helps to build a growing community of women who are like-minded and share similar spirits in terms of wanting to not only succeed but also serve.

What are some common misconceptions women can have about hiring a coach or consulting to help get to the top of their industry?

Kynia Starkey: A common misconception is the belief that it's not worth investing in any type of coach, let alone a life coach. Many cannot wrap their minds around the value it provides and the difference it would make in their life. I also think many feel as if it is difficult to find someone who understands their journey, and so there tends to be some hesitation to invest. Women also have a tendency to not feel they are worthy enough to allot funds for the purpose of investing in themselves but rather in their families. However, it is my mission to dispel these misconceptions by sharing my journey. We want to let women know that they're not alone, we can help them navigate their journey, and that it is worth the investment.

What are some of the most common fears you have seen women business owners have?

Kynia Starkey: I think it's interesting because the fears are the opposite of the misconceptions. While many women believe that it's not worth having a coach or consultant, at the same time, they have a fear of trying to build a business or brand on their own. So, they remain stuck in a place of feeling like they can't do it and remain stagnant because they will not seek help from a coach who can help navigate the journey with them. The fear of failing can be debilitating as well. However, it is essential to understand that they can find success even after failure.

How can they get past these fears?

Kynia Starkey: I encourage women to have faith, which is the total opposite of fear. Faith is built on solid belief and fuels the courage they need to work on developing their businesses, brands, and behind the scenes. I also encourage the women to get into a community that will undergird their faith and help them to push past the fears.

What other perceived obstacles do you see that might be preventing women entrepreneurs from seeking the help of a life coach?

Kynia Starkey: In addition to considering the cost, they may think that they're already too busy to fit in working with a coach. They may also be apprehensive about sharing their challenges with someone they consider a stranger. Others may think they are not good enough, while some are simply afraid of success.

What are some of the little-known pitfalls or common mistakes you see women entrepreneurs make as they attempt to balance life, family, and business?

Kynia Starkey: Not having a practical plan and tools to manage your business, brand, and the behind the scenes are common mistakes women make. It's not just having a business plan, the laid-out goals, and financial forecasts but actually having the high-level and lower-level details. Operating inefficiently can also be a big pitfall. It helps to operate both in the business and behind the scenes efficiently with a streamlined approach using the right tools and techniques effectively.

How can these pitfalls or mistakes be avoided?

Kynia Starkey: Well, as a coaching and consulting service, we help women to hit the ground running. It shortens the length of time that they would have to figure out what tools would be best for their particular businesses. Secondly, just having someone who's experienced with streamlining business operations helps. Additionally, having a mentor that serves as a sounding board and helps them consider alternative solution or helps them see the forest for the trees, so to speak.

Can you share an example of how you helped a woman who you worked with overcome some obstacles she was facing?

Kynia Starkey: I had a female client who was working a day job, but it wasn't the career she desired. She had a lot of business ideas that she wanted to move forward with but felt she didn't have enough time or income to invest in moving them along. She wanted to write a book, record a CD and create an apparel line. During my time as her coach, I helped her build a project plan that consisted of tasks and dates for each idea. We outlined priorities for her, streamlined work processes and identified the additional resources she would need to accomplish each endeavor. At the end of her time with me, we were able to execute all the business ideas while remaining on budget and schedule.

Another woman I worked with was really brilliant at her big-picture vision, but she was drowning in the small details and execution. I started working with her and created systems and processes that were easily repeatable, and she said that it lifted a weight off her shoulders. Each woman I work with needs a different type of support or coaching, and I pride myself on learning what that is.

What inspired you to become a life coach for women?

Kynia Starkey: My past experiences really drive me. I have had experiences with a debilitating illness, gone through two divorces, and I've had other failures in business. I know that those things can be paralyzing if you feel like you're in it alone. The combination of these challenges, and overcoming them, inspires me to help other women navigate their journey and avoid some of the bumps in the road that I had to experience.

It also really lights me up and is very rewarding to share in someone's journey and undergird them, especially through a tough time. Hard times don't last forever!

Can you share a lesson you learned early on in your business journey that still impacts how you do business today?

Kynia Starkey: At the beginning of my career, I didn't have my business set up correctly. I had a lot on my plate, but as I grew in my role as a project manager, I began applying those lessons to my life. Now I'm helping women not to make the same mistakes.

What's the most important question a female entrepreneur should ask herself to determine if she should hire a life coach?

Kynia Starkey: I think women must consider what the cost would be if they continue to do things the same way or the cost of inaction. They should also really evaluate what they may be missing out on if they don't move forward and get some assistance.

What is the benefit of hiring a life coach on one's business journey? And why do you refer to it as a journey?

Kynia Starkey: There are many benefits to hiring a female life coach. There are challenges which are inherent to being a woman, and we have or will all face them at some point, so there is an opportunity to glean from the experience that the coach has as a female. There's also a sense of partnership that comes with having a life coach to ease the journey. Finally, having someone who can provide an outside perspective. These are all benefits of hiring a life coach.

I refer to navigating in business as a journey because we are constantly moving forward in our businesses and in our lives. Building a business or a brand is not a sprint; it's an ongoing process. You don't sprint to success—it's a journey, and it takes time.

What's the most important thing women entrepreneurs should consider when evaluating and selecting a life coach?

Kynia Starkey: I think the well-rounded experience of a life coach is essential. Women should seek out someone that has experience in a multitude of areas and not just one in particular.

What would you say to a woman about the experience they will have by working with you?

Kynia Starkey: I would say that my greatest value as a coach is all the life experiences I have. I leverage my experience in coaching and consulting as well as my years as an employee in corporate America. I have managed schedules and projects for Fortune 500 companies; I have had my own high highs and low lows. I am a single mom, twice divorced and had to learn entrepreneurship after having a comfortable six-figure salary. I have transitioned from corporate America to becoming a busy mompreneur, and I have learned the value of not taking this journey alone as a solopreneur. I've navigated many journeys, and I can help make yours much easier. Lastly, I believe I offer a well-rounded coaching experience because I coach the whole woman—mind, body, and spirit. With my spiritual calling and gift of prayer for healing, I believe I am here to help women walk in their full purpose and potential, which will ultimately enable them to run the most successful business they were put here to share.

About Kynia Starkey

Kynia Starkey has over 20 years of experience in corporate project management, marketing, and business operations. Kynia has worked in global and remote capacities with companies highly renowned in their respective industries, including Sony Music as Global Director of Project Management, The National Basketball Association as Project Manager of NBA and WNBA website development, IBM in various capacities, Pearson Inc. as Implementation Manager, and several successful start-ups. After deciding to throw in the corporate towel, Kynia has become a serial entrepreneur, now specializing in empowering women through her health, wellness, and business initiatives.

Kynia also runs FEM Moguls and the Mogulista Movement, helping female business owners on their journey to the top. In addition to being a speaker, author and life coach, Kynia also offers project management consultation and digital design and marketing services.

She is the creator of Helpful and Healing, a lifestyle initiative that encourages people to live better. Kynia's mission closely aligns with her newly discovered calling of helping women in business experience total freedom, including health, wealth, and wholeness.

WEBSITE

FEMMoguls.mn.co

FACEBOOK

Facebook.com/FEMmoguls

TWITTER

Twitter.com/FEMMoguls

INSTAGRAM

Instagram.com/FEMMoguls

LINKEDIN

LinkedIn.com/in/KyniaStarkey

As a Woman, You Are Uniquely Designed to Succeed – Here's How to Tap into Your Energy and Unleash Your Gift to Grow Your Business Faster Than You Imagined

Have you been struggling to run a profitable business but, in your heart, know you can be unstoppable with the right support? Does your vision feel bigger than you can accomplish on your own? Do you know that you have a unique gift but can't seem to unleash it? There are ways to achieve the results you desire. Deep inside of you, there is energy and a burning desire to do more, be more and achieve more. As a woman, you are innately gifted to succeed.

The models you see for success in business are typically men. Masculine energy tends to be focused on crushing it and hustling. They use unsustainable energy to achieve results. Male energy is different because they have testosterone, and females don't. As a woman, you have to use a more sustainable approach. If you are going to manage your business, you need to market the most unique version of you. You need to stand out, and that means you need to know what your unique gift is. By discovering what your unique gift is, you can learn how to use it and stand out in a very crowded and very complicated market by being the best version of you. As your business grows, you, too, will evolve. That means that when you start your business, you might not be the same when your business grows to the next level. It is important that you continue to evolve as a leader as your business grows, but no matter how big it becomes, it's important that you stay connected to why you started your business in the first place.

If you want to amplify your profits, release the constraints many women put around themselves and tap into your bold mindset, I know you'll find the interview with Melanie Benson enlightening. −Conversation with Lisa C. Williams

Lisa Charlene Williams is the Founder of the #SmartHustle #SmartGrind movement (amiontheverge.com), an initiative to help female entrepreneurs succeed in business and life, stop working themselves to death and become the Doyennes of their industry, a woman who is the most respected or prominent person in a particular field.

Conversation with Melanie Benson

Share about your coaching and consultancy company and how you can specifically help women business owners.

Melanie Benson: My clients come to me with one primary problem. They feel stuck at one level. Their business won't grow, and they feel like they have to give something up. They are very conflicted about how to grow because they have had to sacrifice something important to get to where they are now. So, what we do is create a new set of rules to achieve a new level of success, and ultimately, it's increasing income and impact for most of my clients in a more sustainable line.

What are the advantages of women playing bigger and creating their own rules of success?

Melanie Benson: I believe that women are uniquely designed to bring transformation into our world. We are creators. We are helpers. Women are nimble, and they tend to have unique qualities. They bring change forward, and what they need is to be believed in and to be given the tools to power up and grow.

What do you feel are the biggest myths out there when it comes to a woman playing bigger in her market or in her industry?

Melanie Benson: One of the most common myths is, you have to work more to achieve more. We see that in popular memes that say, "You can sleep when you are dead" or "Get up and hustle and grind." The fear is that if we don't work more, we won't achieve more, when often times it's just that we are using the wrong tool to grow our business.

What are some of the common misconceptions that women business owners have with regard to growing their business?

Melanie Benson: One of the most common misconceptions is that they are going to have to do it alone. They are never going to find anybody who can help them grow it if they can't afford to hire help to grow. I think that mentality often causes you to become very stagnant and experience slow growth. Slow growth can depress you. It can frustrate you. It can make you believe that you are not capable of growing to a bigger level.

Yes, definitely. Your answer kind of goes into the next question with regard to the fears that you have heard and experienced with your clients. Are there any other fears that maybe we didn't talk about yet?

Melanie Benson: There are a lot of fears. A big one is the fear of not being capable. You are afraid to put yourself out there for fear that you might be found to be imperfect or that you don't know everything. I think another one, especially for people who are high achievers, is, they believe they are superheroes and they can do everything. They've achieved a certain level of success for a long time, and they don't want to miss out on anything, so they say yes to everything. Then they become overwhelmed with too many commitments and end up having an unclear brand with too many offerings because they are afraid that they will miss out on something if they can't do it all and that they shouldn't say no.

How do you think they can get past the fears you just mentioned?

Melanie Benson: I think fear is misunderstood. Fear is most often our logical mind trying to come up with a logical way to get somewhere, and if it is not logical, fear takes over. First of all, getting past fear involves recognizing that fear is not a tough time. It's simply a sign you need more information. How are you going to get that information? How are you going to use your mindset differently than you ever have before to achieve things you have never achieved before?

What other perceived obstacles do you see that might prevent female business owners from seeking the help of someone like yourself?

Melanie Benson: Going back to mindset, this is a very common reason why people don't invest in what they want. They've not cultivated what I call a bold mindset, and they've let their perception of their money picture dictate their growth.

Money is a reflection of our resourcefulness. If you are resourceful, you are one hundred percent committed to something. If you are not one hundred percent committed to something, you will be living in limitation, and you will buy into the logical fear of not having enough because you believe that the picture you see is the only picture. When you are ready, because you've committed, and you are all in, it creates a command that you will activate what you want. So, you have to learn to use the magic of bold thinking and the magic of bold action. That is where you uncover things you didn't know were there until you make the commitment and you've decided you are all into something. That's how you get any level of growth you want.

What are one or two little-known pitfalls or common mistakes you see women in business make on the road to growing their business?

Melanie Benson: Two of the biggest are not hiring soon enough and over creating. Creativity is an addictive energy. It is so fun. So, creativity is often what many people lead with, and they think, *If I want to grow my income, I need to create more things.* But what they don't do is, they don't optimize what they have so that the things they've created perform better and generate more profitability. It's a common pitfall that leaves people struggling for more income, eventually suspending all their time and energy creating.

Can you share an example of how you helped a woman you worked with specifically overcome some obstacles and achieve success?

Melanie Benson: Yes, I'll share a couple. I had a woman who is a consultant and researcher. She had a very successful consulting business, but she was overwhelmed, and she was exhausted. She couldn't grow. She hit her income ceiling very prematurely, and she truly believed she had to do it all herself. I helped her uncover a leverage strategy that was aligned with her. I taught her how to hire the people who could actually take things off her plate so she could focus on her unique genius in the business. After putting the team together, learning how to systemize things and putting the right strategies in place for other people to relieve her of common activities, she was able to go from two hundred thousand to a seven-figure business and then start working thirty-hour work weeks.

I worked with another woman who owned a copyrighting company. She was stuck in it and not breaking the six-figure mark. We figured out she was stuck because she didn't have support. Once we figured that out, she started growing and achieving a six-figure income. The key there was: figuring out why she was stuck.

For brick and mortar business owners, I helped an accountant who was making well into six figures, but she had no life. She was very frustrated and overwhelmed. She felt like she didn't want to grow because she didn't want to lose any more time in her life. So, we figured out how to shift what she was focusing on for her revenue producing activity and tried to do something for her that wasn't in revenue by simply refocusing on a higher revenue-generating opportunity that was already in the business.

Melanie, what inspired you to become a coach?

Melanie Benson: I was working in a corporate environment. I'd been there for thirteen years, and I didn't see a future. I started looking for a way to use my gifts in corporate—achieving goals—and monetize it around my own business. That translated into coaching at that time, so I became a coach literally because it was the only skill I knew how to do.

Excellent. What has inspired you to really dig into helping women in business?

Melanie Benson: Well, that was seventeen years ago, and so every day since my evolution, I was more and more inspired to help women because women often times have a lot of built-in limitations from their culture and from their familiar training. I believe that helping women learn the right tools to grow and staying in touch with their unique gifts will help the world become a better place and create more financial abundance on the planet.

Can you share a lesson you learned early on that still impacts you and how you do business today?

Melanie Benson: I struggled to understand my intuition from my fears. I made my biggest mistakes when I pushed aside my intuition and listened instead to someone else's advice. A specific example of that was when I was leaving for Europe fifteen years ago. I realized I needed an assistant because the person I had in that role couldn't do it anymore. I hired someone, even though I was screaming inside knowing she was not the right person. I went off to Europe. When I came back, she had made a real mess of things and then disappeared. Literally, we couldn't find her. Every costly mistake I trace back to not listening to my intuition and not trusting it.

What would you say is the most important question for female entrepreneurs or business owners to ask themselves as they consider working with a company or individual, or should I say hiring a coach?

Melanie Benson: I think it's important to get clarity on where you want to be, and what that's worth to you, and then look at investing in someone who can get you there faster with fewer mistakes. Is the investment worth it to you? For example, one of my mastermind clients always says, "Find out the eighteen thousand dollars. Melanie, that same year, I will make a hundred thousand dollars back in my growth. It's the smartest ever I can make." That's the way we have to think. We have to think about our life; not like this is a cost, and you cannot afford it, but can you afford not to do it?

What would you say is the most important consideration for a woman to think about when evaluating a prospective coach?

Melanie Benson: *Will I allow them to take me where I want to go?* Basically, you have to respect them, and you have to trust them. If you don't respect who they are and the way they operate, and if you don't trust them, you will never let go of the steering wheel and let them help you drive.

In closing, what would you like to leave a female business owner with, regarding what the experience would be like working with you?

Melanie Benson: What I would want for them is to decide if they want to get there faster with fewer bumps. They get to choose if they want to excel at their results or if they want to slowly climb towards those results. When people work with me, they are accelerating.

About Melanie Benson

Melanie Benson (formerly Melanie Strick), a revenue strategist and business performance optimizer, is a guide for conscious entrepreneurs ready to accelerate their impact and income by making their business perform ten times better. With over 12 years of experience in corporate America, Melanie specializes in aligning visionary, game-changing entrepreneurs who are emerging as leaders with the most powerful mindset, actions, and strategies that propel them to a level of success they never knew they could achieve.

Melanie combines her extensive traditional education (she holds a Bachelor's degree in Business Management and a Master's degree in Organizational Management) with multiple advanced certifications in Project Management, Results Coaching, Neuro-Linguistic Programming, and even a license as a Spiritual Counselor to get her clients past their obstacles and into impacting the world in a fulfilling and profitable way.

Melanie is the host of "Amplify Your Success" podcast, serves on the Women Speaker's Association executive team, is the programming chair for the Association of Transformational Leaders and is a co-author of Entrepreneur.com's *Start Up Guide to an Information Marketing Business.*

Melanie speaks for many entrepreneurial audiences across the globe, both live and virtually, via webinars and telephone-based seminars; has been a regularly featured expert on radio shows and in media publications such as American Express *OPEN Forum*, Bloomberg *BusinessWeek*, *Women's Day*, *Parenting* Magazine, University of Phoenix *Alumni* Magazine, and *Female Entrepreneur* Magazine.

WEBSITE
MelanieBenson.com

FACEBOOK
Facebook.com/CoachMelanieBenson

TWITTER
Twitter.com/MelCoach

INSTAGRAM
Instagram.com/CoachMelanieBenson

LINKEDIN
LinkedIn.com/in/Success

Whether You Are Launching or Growing Your Business, Going Through a Transition, or Recreating Your Life, You Need to Connect, Collaborate, and Celebrate with Like-Minded Women

Are you interested in forging new friendships for personal reasons? Are you looking to connect with other professional women and forge alliances with colleagues and possibly clients as well? Do you find yourself wishing you could do more learning and self and professional development? Whether you want to connect with other women who are focused on growing their business or whether you just want to learn and grow, having a community to do so in is key to thriving.

You may be going through a transition. You may be trying to find yourself or redefine your life. You may be striving to recreate your life after experiencing a change in your relationship status. Maybe you're launching your business or trying to grow your business, and you need some support along the way. Or maybe you're doing great, but you don't have much access to meet new people, and you're looking for someone to celebrate your success with. Whatever kind of stress you're under, and whatever season of life you're currently in, whether personally or professionally, you don't have to go through it on your own.

There are communities of women who are facing some of the same things you're facing, who are willing and eager to learn with you, support you, encourage you, and even cry with you when the time calls for it. If you want more information on one such group, I know you'll find the interview with Dr. Marcy Cole enlightening. —Conversation with Lisa C. Williams

Lisa Charlene Williams is the Founder of the #SmartHustle #SmartGrind movement (amiontheverge.com), an initiative to help female entrepreneurs succeed in business and life, stop working themselves to death and become the Doyennes of their industry, a woman who is the most respected or prominent person in a particular field.

Conversation with Dr. Marcy Cole

Share about First Tuesday LA—what the organization is and how you're helping women.

Dr. Marcy Cole: The mission of First Tuesday LA is to create a sense of community through social connectivity, professional networking, and social service. We embrace women of all ages, all walks of life, and we invite them into our community. We have an online network for women all over the world to connect with one another. There's also an online membership providing access to each other to share questions, resources, and invitations—on the personal or professional front. We have live events where we integrate networking and education, featuring a guest speaking about self-development, human potential, and professional development.

The social service piece is that we really attract a very heart-centered community. We don't vet the women who come through the door, but everyone's focus is similar. Like attracts like. First Tuesday attracts a beautiful group of women who care about their community, care about humanity, care about the conditions of the world and how they can be of service.

I feel like the most powerful currency we have is connectivity.

First Tuesday is not a networking group exclusive to business owners or entrepreneurs. It started in living rooms in Chicago just because I love bringing people together.

What would you say the advantages are for a businesswoman to be a part of a community that offers your three pillars of social connection, professional collaboration, and humanitarian service?

Dr. Marcy Cole: The advantages are that everything starts with a relationship. It gives them the opportunity to be outside of their circle of influence—their family, friends, and neighborhood—and get out and meet new people. When you meet new people, you never know where opportunities or synchronies might lie between you or might arise as a result. A stranger might become a sister, a friend, or business partner. She might become a client or customer.

Self-development is a big part of First Tuesday. We have smaller monthly events, the First Tuesday evening of most months with well-known thought leaders speaking, and then we have one annual large event called Epic Day, featuring highly visible influencers, New York Times bestsellers, and international speakers. There's an educational, personal, and professional growth component at this event open to women and men.

This year was my 3rd year producing it, and the speaker line up was amazing, with Jack Canfield, Michael Beckwith, Dr. John Demartini, Rebecca Rosen, and Lisa Nichols.

What would you say are the biggest myths out there when it comes to a woman joining an organization with other women?

Dr. Marcy Cole: Most of us have had the experience in life when we wanted to be included but felt excluded. We all want to be seen, heard, valued, and connected. That's a part of our human nature and one thing we all have in common. So, I think a myth is that sometimes women think that joining a group with other women will result in being catty, cliquey, or competitive. Or introverted women might think they will get overwhelmed if there's too much going on.

The truth is, we have nothing to lose by walking through the door of any place and seeing if it resonates with us and feels in alignment with our energy, values, and heart. When you open yourself up to new experiences, you are open to beautiful surprises, meaningful relationships and a wider lens through which you learn new things and new perspectives. You can grow in whatever domain you're interested in growing.

At First Tuesday, friendships and connections are forged, not cliques. And that's the beauty of community.

What are some common fears that women have regarding social connectivity?

Dr. Marcy Cole: As I mentioned, a common fear is often that they're not going to feel like they belong. They might fear feeling uncomfortable or overwhelmed walking into a room full of strangers in an unfamiliar environment. Sometimes women find themselves intimidated by others, comparing themselves and saying, "Well, I'm not her" or "Gosh, I can't believe what she's doing. Who am I to be here!"

How can they get past those fears?

Dr. Marcy Cole: They can get past those fears by choosing to check their ego at the door and choosing to walk

into a new environment with an open mind and a full heart.
Period. And then see what transpires.

What perceived obstacles do you see that might be preventing women from visiting or considering joining an organization like yours?

Dr. Marcy Cole: I think information overload, busy schedules, or having a lot of options out there to choose from often keeps many people inundated, isolated and tired. This can make them resistant and paralyzed to get out of their own familiar bubble and routine.

What are some of the pitfalls or common mistakes that you see women entrepreneurs make on the road to growing their business?

Dr. Marcy Cole: Common mistakes include adrenal exhaustion because they are not getting enough help. They think they have to grow before they invest, as opposed to investing in help and a team and training so that they can grow. A lot of times, I see women doing it alone versus receiving enough support and welcoming collaboration.

Can you share an example of how you've helped a woman overcome an obstacle she was facing?

Dr. Marcy Cole: Well, it's almost like a prototype because it happens a lot. I saw a woman as a client in my psychotherapy practice who felt overwhelmed as a female entrepreneur doing too much for too long. So, I took her through a few steps. First, I helped her get back to the why—why is she doing her business? Sometimes, when we feel overwhelmed, we forget the inspiration behind why we're doing what we're doing in the first place! The why is the engine, which is what gives us the energy and the drive and the resilience to stick with it, especially when times get tough. Second, I took her through a meditative process where she was able to have some time to reflect and connect with herself again. Third, I helped her create a time management strategy to focus on one goal—one step at a time to get one step closer each day to achieve her vision

The fourth step was to encourage her to find the help that she needed. Over time, her central nervous system calmed down because she got back to what inspired her to launch her business. And because she hired a part-time virtual assistant, instead of feeling stressed out all the time, she began to feel supported ... and stopped feeling so alone and inundated. One thing led to another, and six months later, she was in a very different place. She is now managing a successful business and out of the launch phase grind because of the steps that she took and the investment she made in her own wellbeing.

What inspired you to become a coach for women and to create First Tuesday?

Dr. Marcy Cole: My profession is a holistic psychotherapist. I also do life coaching. That's been my profession for twenty-five years. I pursued this because I felt a calling to support and empower others to find their voice, their truth, share their gifts with the world and be able to receive the fulfilling, joyful life that everyone deserves to receive.

First Tuesday was organic. It was not a contrived business idea at all. As I said earlier, it began in living rooms in Chicago. Women responded, and it grew into a life force of its own.

Now, we have an international online community. We have live events on a monthly basis in Los Angeles. Our EPIC DAY event each year has attracted over 200 attendees and has sold out each year.

Can you share a lesson you learned early on that still affects how you do business today?

Dr. Marcy Cole: The lesson I remember learning early on is: "Don't put off until tomorrow what you can do today." Just do it. Just get the stuff that you don't want to do done. And relationships. I can't stress enough how important those are. Everything comes down to our relationship with ourselves. How good do we feel in our own skin? How connected are we to our truth and our gift? How worthy do we feel to have it all?

Everything also comes down to our relationships with others and the quality of those relationships. Everything stems from that, whether it's in your personal life or your professional life.

What would you say is the most important question a woman should consider when choosing a network or an organization to join to support her and her business?

Dr. Marcy Cole: I think it's about alignment. You want to find a community that is in alignment with your values, your vision, your offerings, what you want to receive, what you want to share and give. So, the question to explore is, what community IS in alignment with your highest good and the good of all of those around you? I mean, if that's our prayer for the day and intention, the field usually shows up with the exact people we need to meet at the perfect time. It's only when we're not paying attention that we can stray, detour and lose sight of that.

In closing, what would you like to leave a woman with who might be considering attending a First Tuesday gathering? What would the experience be like?

Dr. Marcy Cole: Connection, collaboration, and celebration. I'd love for her to walk in curious and open. And I'd love for her to walk out feeling full, energized, inspired and connected ... to more of herself and connected with others in that room who were strangers before she walked through the door. I'd like her to look back one day and remember that first First Tuesday event when she met some of her lifelong friends.

About Marcy Cole, Ph.D.

Dr. Marcy Cole is a psychotherapist, writer, speaker, community mobilizer and humanitarian visionary.

Dr. Cole's practice serves adolescents, adults, and couples. Her treatment approach is holistic, focusing on supporting optimal physical, mental, emotional and spiritual health in the clients she serves. She sees clients in Marina del Rey and Westwood, CA, and offers virtual consultation.

As an author, Dr. Cole's published doctoral dissertation is a qualitative study on "The Experiences of Never-Married Women from the Ages 29–39 Who Desire Marriage and Children." She is a best-selling co-author of *Living Proof: Celebrating the Gifts that Came Wrapped in Sandpaper* and *Get Your Woman On: Embracing Beauty, Grace and the Power of Women*. Dr. Cole is also a blog author for *The Huffington Post*, *Thrive Global*, and *Goop*.

Dr. Cole has been featured as an expert on television shows such as Dr. Drew's *Lifechangers* on the CW Network, *Millionaire Matchmaker* on Bravo, *Braxton Family Values* on WE Network, and *Issues with Jane Valez-Mitchell* on HLN. She also produces live and online programing for First Tuesday LA, creating a sense of community through social connectivity, professional networking, and social service.

In the fall of 2011, Dr. Cole launched an online platform for women without children, whether by choice or circumstance, called Childless Mothers Connect, honoring the 'mother' in every woman. She also founded CMomA.org, promoting the connection between people without children and children in need. CMomA's programing is now a part of KidSave.org.

WEBSITE
DrMarcyCole.com

FACEBOOK
Facebook.com/DrMarcyCole

TWITTER
Twitter.com/MarcyColePhD

LINKEDIN
Linkedin.com/in/Marcy-Cole-ph-d-1a89107/

Are You Struggling to Bring Visibility, Value, and The Right Messaging to Your Business or Brand? Learn the Key to Getting Ahead in Life and Business

If you are struggling to bring visibility, value, placement, and the right messaging to your business brand, the answer to your struggle might not be to invest in more strategizing but rather to invest in support. Are you tired of not having a seat at the table? If so, the answer to your tiredness might be to create your own table and invite other women to have a seat at it. You will be amazed at how quickly it spreads and how readily relationships are formed that will last for years to come.

In business, women often talk about supporting one another but rarely do they back up their words with action. Whether you're a wife and mother or single but doing amazing things in business, you need the support of other like-minded women. You need to affirm one another's power and celebrate each other's achievements. By taking the time to connect on a deeper level and get to know someone else's story, you will find out that in business, every woman needs support, regardless of how successful or experienced she is.

When you develop stronger friendships with other women and invest in connecting and learning from those friendships, you will be able to get more things done and go farther, faster—not just in your professional life but in your personal life as well. If you want more information on how to nurture and develop stronger relationships, both with people you already know and with new people, I know you'll find Nikkia McClain's interview helpful. −Conversation with Lisa C. Williams

Lisa Charlene Williams is the Founder of the #SmartHustle #SmartGrind movement (amiontheverge.com), an initiative to help female entrepreneurs succeed in business and life, stop working themselves to death and become the Doyennes of their industry, a woman who is the most respected or prominent person in a particular field.

Conversation with Nikkia McClain

Share about your new initiative, #Support Your Girlfriend.

Nikkia McClain: #SupportYourGirlfriend is an initiative I created last summer to bring women in business together. As women, we all deal with ups and downs as it relates to family, clients, and even colleagues. I wanted to create an initiative for women; as they are going through life and business, they always know that they have those Girlfriends who they can call on. It could just be to talk about their day when they need support. It's having that sister or sisters in the room to cheer you on. It means a lot when you have women who are genuinely present in your life to encourage you and to push you forward.

And as they support you, you are in turn able to support them. There are three concepts under my #SupportYourGirlfriend initiative: SupportHER, which means being there with them as they launch their product, service, or brand. Or when she's having a rough day, it may involve being available for her to call you and talk to you about what's going on, and you just reminding that sister friend how amazing they are and how important their role is. CelebrateHER is just that celebrating that sister friend through all the amazing milestones going on for her in life; it could be a new job, role at work, new baby, wedding, and any other endeavors. Lastly, Pow(H)er is to empower your sister friend.

In your opinion, what are the advantages for women entrepreneurs in developing stronger friendships and connecting and learning from them?

Nikkia McClain: I believe a key advantage for women entrepreneurs developing friendships is that you would be more capable of getting things done. When you connect, learn, and seek to develop stronger relationships by forming friendships with women, you are able to do a lot more. You also go further in connecting with women, as opposed to viewing them as competition and falsely thinking that you can't work with them. I definitely love connecting, learning from, and developing stronger friendships with people who I know in business. It allows me to accomplish a lot more in life, as opposed to always turning my nose up at other women because I feel like I can't work with them. I don't believe in that notion.

What do you feel are the biggest myths out there when it comes to women connecting? What have you heard?

Nikkia McClain: For me, as a woman of color, how difficult it is to work with another woman of color. I'm like: "What do you mean I can't work with any woman, especially when she is a sister?" If a woman goes into a place feeling like they can't get along with a person, then those are the same vibes that they are going to get back in return. Some of the strongest relationships that I've formed in business have been with women, so I believe that the idea that women cannot work effectively with other women is a complete myth.

What are some common misconceptions about women entrepreneurs getting together outside of business and the effectiveness of them doing so?

Nikkia McClain: Well, I think a lot of women do see a business relationship only as a business relationship. I'm not against anyone having that viewpoint; however, I've been able to form wonderful friendships out of my business relationships. So, oftentimes, I and the people who I work with do get together to have a cocktail or two—okay, maybe three or four—and talk about what's going on in our lives.

There are those women who say, "No, I keep my business relationship my business relationship." Sometimes, you need to do that, but I also think that by doing so, you risk restricting yourself from getting to know the woman in business who you work with pretty much on a consistent basis. You risk missing more than a relationship but a friendship that could evolve out of that.

What would you say are some of the most common fears women have about developing stronger friendships or relationships?

Nikkia McClain: Common fears women have about developing stronger relationships boils down to confidence. I think women sometimes lack confidence when it comes to relating to other strong, like-minded women, and that can be fearful.

When you see someone who is very confident, it can make you feel like you are not as confident. Such a feeling is not necessary, but that's the fear that women often have. They think that another woman who is just as driven as them may get ahead, faster than they do, leaving them to deal with the feeling that they are not enough to be in a friendship with that person. That is one common fear.

The way they can get past that fear is by being okay with who they are. Sometimes it's awkward, even for me, when I go into a room and meet a woman for the first time, but I have to push past that fear and be determined to meet someone new. I have to be determined to develop a relationship with whomever I want to connect with. To develop strong relationships, the key for women is to push past their fears. They just have to tell themselves: "You know what, there's nothing to be fearful of. If the person rejects or doesn't immediately take a liking to me, so what!"

What perceived obstacles do you see that might be preventing women entrepreneurs from hiring and working with someone like you?

Nikkia McClain: I don't face much of a challenge when it comes to a woman hiring me or me hiring another woman. I'm very invested in those who work for me, and my goal has always pushed them to learn from me, achieve their best potential and be better than me. I think one obstacle is that some people are not okay with women getting things done, but that's not the case for me. I'm always encouraging other women to take the initiative. I want their successes to be better than mine, which means we are both pushing one another along.

Based on working with women in the past, what are some of the common mistakes that female entrepreneurs make on the road to growing their business?

Nikkia McClain: One mistake that women make is developing a relationship and then not nurturing that relationship. They often meet someone and try to figure out immediately: *What can you do for me?* That's not how any relationship works. You must nurture that relationship. By doing so, it becomes beneficial down the line. In my line of work, I see women attach themselves to different things or people just for the sake of pushing ahead, without really having a good understanding of who that person is and really getting to know what they are about.

Can you share an example of how you've helped a woman you've worked with and how you enhanced her business?

Nikkia McClain: Absolutely. We had an amazing client who was gearing up for the release of her first book. I told her, "Listen. I don't want you to do a regular book tour where you show up, and people come in to hear you speak about the book, read an excerpt from the book, take a photo with you, then you sign a copy of that book, and that's it. Such a book tour is not going to be beneficial to your brand, and it's definitely not going to be beneficial to you. You are very personable, and I want women to fall in love with you."

We decided to create a Glam Night Out, which turned out to be very successful for both the book and her personal brand. We did a seven-city tour, and for the purpose of the book tour, women came together and got complementary beauty services in return for purchasing the book. In addition, each city that we went to, we honored women, two to three women. It was great. The women loved it. The people who were honored were so happy to be honored, but most importantly, when the events were over, it enhanced my client's personal brand.

What inspired you to become a marketing and public relations specialist?

Nikkia McClain: I had no background in public relations. I came into public relations on faith. I was in real estate and did party promotions on the side for extra money. While doing a New Year's Event, I was approached by a fashion designer who was blown away by how I laid out the event for my client. She came up to me and said, "I want you to be my publicist." I was like, "Your publicist?" So, that encounter spurred me to find out what a publicist is. Then, I later on went to my husband and told him that I was going to start my own public relations firm. That was seven years ago, and I've been going hard ever since.

Can you share a lesson that you learned early on that still impacts how you do business today?

Nikkia McClain: Absolutely. To remain consistent and efficient. When I started out in public relations, I made a lot of mistakes, but that was okay because I learned from those mistakes. I don't make those same mistakes today, so it forces me to remain consistent and my work be efficient. My other lesson would be: respect your relationships. I am always trying to be resourceful for my clients, which means that I take my time getting to know someone and build on that relationship. In my line of business, I can pitch clients all day long, but if I don't have the necessary or the proper relationships, things won't come to fruition for me and my clients.

What would you say is the most important question women entrepreneurs should ask themselves as they consider who they work with to enhance their brand?

Nikkia McClain: The first question they need to ask themselves is: *By working with this person or with this particular service, does it tarnish my own brand?* I don't do anything that I think will hinder or hurt my own brand.

What's the most important thing women entrepreneurs should consider when evaluating joining a group, organization, or community?

Nikkia McClain: I think the first thing that they need to consider is if it brings them value. There are a lot of organizations that pop up for people to be a part of, but I feel that many times organizations benefit from the fees that members are paying without really delivering anything of value. So, I would encourage women to ask if joining a group, organization, or community, does it bring them or their brand value? Does it enhance their growth? That growth does not only have to be their career growth but also could be their personal growth. Women should ask: "Does joining enhance me or my brand, and does it allow me to grow—either personally or professionally?"

What would you say to a female entrepreneur about what the experience would be like for her if she attended one of your events?

Nikkia McClain: I would say the experience is going to be everlasting. Like with my #SupportYourGirlfriend initiative, it forced women to evolve and expand on their relationships.

For example, one of the young ladies who attended had recently gone through a divorce, but if you spoke to her today, you would have no idea. We've been working hard and pushing her own brand forward. She is part of many initiatives with my firm, but most importantly, I gained a friend.

During one conversation we had together, this young lady said, "Nikkia, I can't believe where my life is at right now." So, I would say that women are sure to evolve working with me or working with my organization.

About Nikkia McClain

Nikkia McClain attended Metropolitan College of New York, where she obtained a bachelor's degree in business administration. In her former career, she worked as a very successful real estate agent. As an agent, she managed million-dollar properties before establishing her own marketing and public relations firm, TENÉ NÍCOLE.

After several years of helping clients realize their real estate dreams, she wanted to explore other opportunities that were also in line with her personal dreams. After being approached by several individuals to manage their businesses, she decided her next move would be to pursue a career in marketing and public relations. A very bold decision without having any background in the two fields. However, she put her knowledge and creative skills to work immediately, carving out her path to becoming successful.

Stepping out on faith, she formulated TENÉ NÍCOLE, an unorthodox and strategic move that has been the most rewarding and the most heartfelt part of her professional career of service. Having raised the level of conversation and opportunities for clients and garnered them publicity in several television, magazine, and radio spots, her efforts continue to maximize the level of exposure clients receive on a national and international level.

Since pursuing her dream of "building my very own well-known recognized brand," she has experienced success after success. With features in *Black Enterprise* Magazine as a "PR Maven." Her firm has represented a roster of past and current clients like: James Anderson (Veteran NFL Player), Darrin Dewitt Henson (Actor), Leslie Lopez (Actress), Josh Xantus (Recording Artist), Carissa Rosario (International Model/Actress), April Woodard (TV Correspondent), Deja 'DejaVu' Carter (Media Personality), Motivational Speaker Lucinda Cross' ACTIVATE Conference, LASIO, Professional Hair Care, Keratin Lounge, Posh Beauty Bar, Tresses by Posh, ARI, Luxury Men's Wear, Kollide TV, Best Selling Author Koereyelle DuBose, Tech Innovator Angel Rich, Rutgers University, and recently signed award-winning beauty brand Mielle Organics in addition to a vast number of recurring clients that work with TENÉ NÍCOLE Marketing and Public Relations on project-based events.

Nikkia graduated in 2016 with a master's degree from George Washington University Graduate School of Political Management and is always looking to make a bigger impact in the field of Marketing and Public Relations. She is married and the proud mother of four wonderful children.

WEBSITE
TeneNicole.com

FACEBOOK
Facebook.com/Tené-Nícole-185095938187866

TWITTER
Twitter.com/TeneNicolePR

INSTAGRAM
Instagram.com/NikkiaMcClain

LINKEDIN
Linkedin.com/in/Nikkia-McClain-17a8a715/

Ladies, Do You Realize That Higher Paying Clients and Customers Are Available to You Right Now Because You Are a Women-Owned Business?

Are you a female business owner that owns at least 51% of your company? Are you ready to strengthen your business profile and move the needle forward in your business?

Believe it or not, hundreds of major U.S. corporations and federal, state, and local government entities desire to work with women-owned businesses. If you're a woman who owns at least 51% of your company, you could greatly benefit from the Women's Business Enterprise Council certification. Before you say "Certification is not for me," continue reading.

Whether you are a consultant, have a product or service, or are just starting a business, getting certified will benefit your business. For small to medium size businesses, B2B and potential partnerships amongst members alone would give you more exposure and enhance your business. There is no better time than now to consider additional avenues for expanding and growing your business. There is a benefit for any woman business owner to get certified by WBENC, even if it's the prestige that comes with attaching your brand to theirs.

All members have access to thousands of corporations representing America's most prestigious brands to connect with and present their products and services to. The goal is to ensure that women business owners have access to the education, support, and tools they need to grow and succeed. If what your business provides can benefit a corporation, retail or government agency and has the capacity to deliver a quality level on large contracts, WBENC certification is a must for you!

Imagine how it could change your business if you were a part of a community of hundreds of thousands of business-women across the country who you could collaborate with, do business with as well as have direct access to and an open door to a current list of supplier diversity and procurement executives who want to do business with you.

If you want to learn how being a part of this growing national organization with chapters in every state can help you go to the next level, I know you'll find the interview with Pamela Williamson enlightening. —Conversation with Lisa C. Williams

Lisa Charlene Williams is the Founder of the #SmartHustle #SmartGrind movement (amiontheverge.com), an initiative to help female entrepreneurs succeed in business and life, stop working themselves to death and become the Doyennes of their industry, a woman who is the most respected or prominent person in a particular field.

Conversation with Dr. Pamela Williamson

Share about the Women's Business Enterprise National Council and how you help female business owners grow their businesses.

Dr. Pamela Williamson: I am the president and CEO of WBEC-West. My region covers Southern California, Utah, Wyoming, Arizona, Colorado, Nevada, Hawaii, and Guam. We expose women business owners to opportunities that they otherwise wouldn't have the opportunity to learn about.

I think the first thing that you achieve by becoming certified with WBENC is, you become a part of the family. I know that sounds a little silly, but in becoming a part of the family, you automatically get the sisterhood of the 1,600 WBEs in the West region who have gone through similar experiences. We also offer a plethora of services, so we've been very fortunate to build strategic alliances with several corporations where they have customized mentorship programs for us. You have an opportunity to apply to participate in a regional mentorship program, but you also have an opportunity to apply for mentorship programs that are national in scope. Finally, we have educational programs that you can come through by being a WBENC certified WBE. You automatically have a team of insiders with some supplier diversity professionals that are really your advocates inside of each corporation. I don't know of any other organization that has that large of a network of corporate advocates who are fighting on the inside, trying to help you attain contracts.

Our expertise as an organization helps you connect the dots between women-owned businesses and opportunities with corporate America, and we do that in a variety of ways. One way is through education. We provide education for women and businesses regarding how to leverage their status of being a WBE through supplier diversity. We walk our women through how to build sustainable relationships with buyers and procurement entities, and we also provide matchmaking opportunities that give businesses much bigger opportunities, which means that we connect women and businesses based on their skills, products, and services. Corporations who are looking to procure these skills, products, or services will do that strategically, where we have corporations select those women that meet their minimum requirements and set up one-on-one meetings with them. We also do sessions that are non-strategic, which allow our women and businesses to connect with corporations that they want to do business with that may not have an opportunity for them at that moment in time.

The next time that you go into a Wal-Mart, pay attention to the tags on some of the products. You'll notice that some have a women-owned tag—products with this tag are made by women who are certified within the WBENC business enterprises.

What are some advantages to getting certified as a women-owned business?

Dr. Pamela Williamson: There are many advantages to being WBENC certified, but I will share four: (1) You are getting a network of women-owned businesses that have gone through similar experiences; (2) You get the opportunity to access our database of eager representatives looking to connect with you; (3) You get to participate in regional and national educational programs and participate in regional and national matchmaker sessions; and (4) you get to collaborate with thousands of women-owned businesses to discuss opportunities to go into larger contracts and to do business with other women all around the country.

For those women-owned businesses that are not quite the size and scope to do business with a major corporation, we've helped several connect the dots with other WBEs and also with second and third tier opportunities. An example of a business certified by WBENC is PC Links, LLC. Tammy Lienhart is the CEO, and her company provides boutique procurement service for those one-off items that corporations are looking for and don't want to buy a million of them. For example, they're looking to replace one headset. That's a product that she provides to corporations that are small volume sales. We additionally have WBEs that do consulting services across the United States.

What are the biggest myths you find that women business owners have about getting certified?

Dr. Pamela Williamson: The number one myth women business owners have about getting certified is that it's extremely difficult or expensive. This is because they don't understand the value of going through the process or the value of certification.

They also don't understand how to leverage the WBENC certification, and that's not something you learn until you get certified. It's difficult to teach someone how to use a certification they don't have yet. But once you are certified, there are several opportunities to connect and learn from other WBEs, corporations, and the WBEC-WEST Staff.

Another myth is that you have to be a mid-size or larger business. Our program can help a woman who is a small business owner get more exposure. Corporations search our portal to locate WBEs that provide products and services, regardless of how big or small that company is. Also, WBEs can search for other WBEs that they want to do business with. You're also able to form partnerships and alliances as a WBENC Certified WBES. You might not be big enough to go after a larger contract, but by joining forces with other WBEs, you can go after that contract.

What are some common misconceptions about getting certified?

Dr. Pamela Williamson: Many women feel that once they get certification, corporations are going to come to them and offer contracts. If you get a gym membership, you have to go into the gym and work out; you're not going to lose any weight if you don't use the equipment. This is the same for certification. You get the certification, and you have to get connected, attend the event and connect with people within the network to really build those relationships.

Another misconception I've heard is women thinking that we are a program like a NAWBO or a women's business center, but there are two main differences in our approach. One is that we do certification, and so we're a certified body. The second is the relationship that we have with corporations.

What are some fears women have regarding certification?

Dr. Pamela Williamson: One fear I have heard is the submission of one's financials. I am really committed to helping women understand why we look at their documents to make a determination. Many business owners, male or female, don't understand the value of their documents. A lot of the reasons for denial are in those organizational documents. There are many instances that after reviewing the organizational documents of a company, it shows that a female owner really doesn't control her business. If you insist that you control it, we want to make sure that the documents confirm that.

Another fear I've heard is around the site interview (visit) component of the certification process. Most of the women who apply truly believe that they own their company and have nothing to hide. For those that are truly women-owned, it's not a big fear.

What other perceived obstacles have you seen women have that might prevent them from getting certified and seeking help from a regional partner like yourself?

Dr. Pamela Williamson: I think a lot of women business owners think they are too small or they can't take full advantage of what's being offered. People sometimes think it's a lot of work when it really isn't.

We spend time with potential WBEs. We walk them through the process and talk with them about where they see their product or service so they can identify whether certification is right for them. Also, we have community partners that help women develop their business and growth plans, especially if it's a startup.

What are pitfalls or common mistakes you see women business owners make on the road to growing and scaling their business?

Dr. Pamela Williamson: Growing and scaling is hard. People underestimate how hard it is. They don't plan as well as they should. The worst case is to get a contract and not be able to scale in order to fulfill that contract. Also, secure capital before you need it. The worst thing is when, 90 days before a contract is going to execute, you're trying to run around and find funding. Always have access to capital. Get it when you don't need it, not when you do.

The way to avoid these pitfalls is to know your market. Before you talk to a corporation, you need to know what solution you're bringing to the table or what problem you're solving. Be the expert. One of the biggest things I hear at a trade show is, "I can do anything that you want. I can provide all things." Well, you probably can't, but you can help that organization grow. You also have to know what's keeping their CEO up at night and have a solution. Compel them to discuss it, hand you their business card, or schedule an appointment. What you have to say is so powerful if you've done your research on that company.

Can you share an example of how you've helped a woman get certified?

Dr. Pamela Williamson: We had a company that was denied before. She said she owned, operated and controlled 51% or more of the company. But upon getting denied, going through the appeals process and talking to her about what we saw in the file, she realized that although she had 51% of the shares, a lot of those shares were no longer voting shares. As such, she didn't really control 51% of the company anymore. Those 'aha' moments are amazing. To go back and do whatever they need to do within their document and come back around, it's just a great feeling.

The one that comes to mind is Deanna Edwards. Her company is called INTU Corporation, and she provides massage therapists for the gaming industry. If you have watched the Super High Roller Bowl, you'll see her team giving individual massages to the players, and they operate 24/7 inside casinos as well. It's been very interesting watching how her company has grown through certification and being able to support her through that. Making those types of introductions and then seeing contracts come out of it at the end has been a great experience. And she's just one example, but I think for me as an individual, she was probably one of the first women who I met when I took on this job, and just watching her grow has been an amazing experience for me personally.

What inspired you to become the president and CEO of the Western region?

Dr. Pamela Williamson: I was working as a Vice President at a behavioral healthcare organization. When my father got sick, I took a sabbatical. A headhunter called me to see if I was interested in applying for the position. Seven interviews later, I learned about supplier diversity and the impact that it makes. In health care, you're not exposed to that. It's a very male-dominated world, especially at that level. I loved learning about the organization and the impact it has on women, the economy, and the community. It's so powerful to help women businesses grow. The more I learned, the more I liked the job. I was very blessed that they selected me.

Can you share a lesson you learned early on that still impacts how you do business today?

Dr. Pamela Williamson: I learned to always make sure I run my decisions through my internal value system. I still do that today. At WBEC-West, my decisions are made through the organization's mission, vision, and value. I make sure I'm ethically and morally okay before moving forward.

What's the most important question a woman business owner should ask themselves when they are considering certification?

Dr. Pamela Williamson: Is their product or service something that they can see in a corporate environment? If you only want to do business with your neighbor, we're probably not a good fit for you.

What's the most important consideration a woman-owned business should think about when evaluating a certification program?

Dr. Pamela Williamson: It's important for them to verify that the organization is nationally recognized. Look at who their corporate sponsors are. When you look at their corporate sponsor list, if you see people you want to do business with on that list, then go back and make sure that the certification body is recognized as one that the corporation accepts and look at the reputation of the certification entity to make sure they're considered the gold standard of certification for women-owned businesses.

What would you like to leave a woman business owner to think about if she decides to go through your certification process? What would you enclose?

Dr. Pamela Williamson: The WBENC certification process is a three-pronged process. First, you have to collect all the documents that are required and upload them into the WBENC portal. After that, our staff reviews those documents. The documents then go to a committee made up of our corporate representative, community partners, and other WBEs. Your file is then reviewed. Once approved, a trained site visitor will visit your business, interview you, and make a determination. Based on the determination from the community and the findings of your site visits, the company is either certified or denied.

One of the biggest problems for women is access. You can have an amazing product or skill, but if you can't get to the right people, it gets very little exposure. Being involved with WBENC allows for a broader exposure, and corporations can go into the WBENC system and find you. It also provides contact information, which makes connections faster and cheaper.

In closing, there are a lot of opportunities to connect and engage through our training. They range from developing your marketing plan to doing business with the government and different industries. Last year alone, we had 197 workshops in our territory—both in-person and webinar trainings. Each one of our states has at least a quarterly event and normally three to four webinars/workshops a month.

We do most of our training for free, or we charge modestly. WBEC-WEST also holds an annual three-day conference with around 100 different corporate procurement professionals and 300–400 WBEs. The cost for certification and filing fees is based on your annual revenue and can range anywhere from $350 to $1,500.

The time frame from submission to acceptance, if an applicant is accepted, can be anywhere from 90 to 180 days, but it depends on whether the applicant submits all the documentation. The ultimate goal of most of our women is to get a corporate contract, expand upon an existing contract, or gain a new contract.

The outcome and business growth of getting a corporate contract and being a certified member of WBENC can be compared to walking around a track without hurdles. There's no maze involved with finding the right person to talk to a corporation. We are able to knock some of those barriers down so that you can grow faster.

About Dr. Pamela Williamson

Dr. Pamela Williamson has been in senior leadership for over 25 years, including three years as CEO of SABA, seven at a business consulting firm, four years as the Vice President of a national behavioral health care organization, and three years as a Deputy Director overseeing the quality control of psychiatric urgent care facilities. Dr. Williamson's areas of expertise lie within change management and reorganization strategies. Dr. Williamson has taken three organizations through a reorganization process in which all organizations turned around fiscally and programmatically utilizing mission-driven, customer-focused servant leadership concepts which resulted in creating highly efficient sustainable environments.

Dr. Williamson is currently the President and CEO of WBENC-West. WBENC-West's mission is to cultivate sustainable relationships between certified women business enterprises and corporate America through certification, education, and targeted networking. In her role as President, she strives to facilitate mutually beneficial procurement opportunities for WBEs and corporations on both a local and national level.

Dr. Williamson holds a doctorate in Healthcare Administration, a Master's in Business Administration, and bachelor's degrees in both social work and psychology. She co-authored the book, *Minority and Women Business Enterprise Certification Levels Playing Field*, and authored the books, *Diverse Supplier Conference Success Guide* and *How to Obtain and Maintain Corporate Contract - 18 Actionable Tips*.

Dr. Williamson resides in Queen Creek, Arizona, with her husband, Ben, and two daughters, Alexandria and Skyler.

WEBSITE
wbec-west.com

Ladies: Ready to Stop Trading Time for Money, Retire Comfortably and Make Money Without Having to Grind?

Have you ever found yourself wondering, *Is my current job or business going to allow me to live the life I desire in 10 years?* Or do you find yourself wanting to make more money but don't have the bandwidth to learn something new or add any more time to your schedule? As women, we are always torn between family and career and struggle to find the right balance between the two. We want to provide for our family, but at the same time, we want to love what we do, have the freedom we desire and make enough money to live comfortably. That can seem impossible at times because there are only 24 hours in a day. Do you think that you are spending too much time working but not getting the compensation you feel you deserve for your time? Take a moment and ponder this question, "What do all the wealthiest people in the world have in common?" The answer? To invest in something that gives them a 'passive income stream'—real estate. No matter what their industry is, no matter what they do.

Real estate allows you to stop trading time for money. As women, we operate differently than men. We run our businesses differently, and freedom may be more important to us. Having a real estate investor mentor that specializes in working with women and who uses language that resonates with you can be just what you need to open your mind to considering real estate investing as a passive stream of income. It will allow you to invest like a lady and get the freedom you desperately desire.

Imagine the possibility of being able to maximize your time while earning a substantial income while you work your current job or run your business? Can you picture what that would mean for your family, for yourself? You'd be able to wake up every day, live your life as you do now and be building a retirement income that doesn't steal time away from you. You will gain a community and sisterhood of women while creating a passive income stream for yourself. If you want to learn more about becoming a real estate investing goddess, I know you'll find the interview with Monick Halm enlightening. −Conversation with Lisa C. Williams

Lisa Charlene Williams is the Founder of the #SmartHustle #SmartGrind movement (amiontheverge.com), an initiative to help female entrepreneurs succeed in business and life, stop working themselves to death and become the Doyennes of their industry, a woman who is the most respected or prominent person in a particular field.

Conversation with Monick Halm

Share about the Real Estate Investor Goddess and how you're helping women with your program.

Monick Halm: It's called the Real Estate Investor Goddesses Wealth Builders Program, and it's a three-month-long program specifically for women. It's an online webinar, and at the end, we have a one-day mastermind in Los Angeles, an in-person get together.

I was inspired to create this program after attending a real estate investing conference with hundreds of people, but only nine were women. I thought: *Let me change this. I want to see more women in the room.* I am so passionate about this because real estate can solve a lot of problems. It allows for true financial freedom. It offers a passive income that can easily cover your expenses, fund your desires and can eventually replace your paycheck.

What are the advantages of women creating real wealth? Describe at least one big problem investing in real estate solves.

Monick Halm: It helps you get your time back and gives you financial freedom. You're able to work when you choose to. You can work on something that's important to you or not work at all. I have a desire to help women learn about real estate to help them get in a financial position to do the work they were born to do, to really live their purpose.

In terms of the problems it can solve, real estate investing can solve a lot of problems, but the main one is that for a lot of women, it solves the problem of feeling like they're on a hamster wheel with work and they do not see a way out. Many women are looking at their future and retirement, and they may not even be sure that they can retire. Some are stuck in their job. Real estate investing is a way to solve all those challenges. You should be having your money work for you to enable you to have more freedom both financially and time-wise. Real estate allows you to replace your paycheck with passive income.

I'm trying to get people to move their money from Wall Street to Main Street, where it helps investors and helps the local community to thrive. At Real Estate Investor Goddesses, we're about investing in property in a way that we leave our properties and communities better than we found them. We're only engaging in a win-win transaction when we ensure that everyone wins in everything we do. Every transaction places a deliberate ripple effect of good in the community.

Real estate investing, however, is not just for people who need to make additional income. There are a lot of people who invest in real estate not because they need more income. They have plenty of income, but they're investing in real estate because they can reduce their taxes. A friend of mine, who is a very successful business owner, found himself with a $500,000 tax bill in one year. Then he found out that by investing in real estate, he could pay substantially fewer taxes even while making more income. He was able to buy an apartment building. The investment helped him greatly reduce his tax burden. I don't know anything about Donald Trump's taxes because he hasn't released them, but I would not be surprised if he legally pays no taxes. He has achieved some great financial success as a real estate investor. So, investing in real estate can be a big benefit for people who don't enjoy giving Uncle Sam any more than they need to. These huge tax advantages also just got even better since the bill passed in December 2017. Those are some of the many benefits of real estate investing.

What are the biggest myths out there when it comes to investing in real estate?

Monick Halm: One of the myths is that you need to have a lot of time or you need to have a lot of money.

There are a lot of busy professional women who'd love to invest in real estate, but they don't have the time to look for a place by themselves. They don't want to deal with the 3 T's: Tenants, Toilets, and Termites. They can invest without having to deal with that as passive investors. I do something called syndication. I bring a group of investors together to collectively purchase larger properties. The passive investors put in the money, and I put in the time to put together the deal and manage the asset, and we all share in the profits.

There are so many ways to invest in real estate. You can invest time, money/credit, relationships, and experience. At least one of those four things are necessary to begin investing in real estate, but you don't necessarily need to have all of them. You can partner with others who do.

What are some misconceptions that you notice women have when it comes to being a real estate investor? What are some general real estate misconceptions?

Monick Halm: A lot of women think they have to do it by themselves. That's a big misconception that will definitely keep a lot of women from making any progress at all because you can't do it alone. Real estate is truly a team sport.

Another big misconception about real estate investing is that you need to have a lot of time or you need to have a lot of money. Regarding time, I know that there are a lot of busy professional women who would love to invest in real estate, but they don't have the time to look up the place by themselves or they don't have the time to deal with tenants, so they shy away from the whole idea of real estate investing. You don't have to invest that way. There are plenty of hands-off opportunities that require little to no time other than educating yourself about the project, which is something I highly recommend.

What I mean by hands-off is that somebody else is doing the work. You can leverage OPT, other people's time, put in some money and then just kick back. There are also ways of investing where you can leverage other people's money, and you don't have to use as much of your own. You can also partner and share in the profit. That's how I invest mostly right now. It's how I've been able to get into over a thousand units. I invest my time and expertise, and others invest their money. Some people have more money than time, so it's a win-win.

What are some common fears?

Monick Halm: I think the biggest fear is that women are afraid that they'll lose money. They're afraid that they're going to be swindled. That's the biggest fear that keeps women from taking action. The best way to get past those fears is education. The more you know, the more you'll be able to spot what is a good investment and what isn't.

Educating yourself about what you are doing is super important. It's the first step anyone should take, but don't learn and then relax. You should continue to learn more about what you are investing in so you can take effective action.

If a woman who is considering investing in real estate can keep these two things in mind, she will always do well:

1. Get educated. You do this by getting under the tutelage of an experienced real estate investor who not only teaches but is actively investing today. The more you know, the more you'll be able to determine what is a good investment and what isn't. Education really will help you feel more confident. Having a mentor, having somebody to help you avoid mistakes, and there will be mistakes. There will be failures. It's not about avoiding all of them, but you can avoid a lot more when working with an experienced investor.

2. Get with a group you resonate with. I think for women having a sisterhood and being a part of a community of women who are investing, learning and growing their portfolios together is important. Developing friendships with women who have your back and who you can grow together with are the things that I think will help women get past that fear. That's why I have created a community of women investors at Real Estate Investor Goddesses— this sisterhood is really supportive of the women in the group.

What are some common mistakes and pitfalls that people investing in real estate experience when they first start investing?

Monick Halm: I know I've said this before, but I can't stress enough how important it is to get a real estate investing education first. Jumping in and investing without being educated and not really knowing what you're doing is a recipe for failure. A pitfall is not having your end game in mind. You have to think about where you want to be, so I like to tell my clients to start with the end in mind.

Remember that real estate investing is not one size fits all. You have to create a clear and personalized real estate investment strategy. This is something that I help my clients to create.

When it comes to women, in particular, we tend to believe that we have to invest by ourselves. That we alone have to protect our money. That's a big misconception and one that would definitely keep a lot of women from making any progress at all because you can't do it alone. Real estate is truly a team sport. You need other people. Even if you're buying your property yourself, you'll still need an agent or broker and an insurance person. You need a team, and women are already wired to work together and to be collaborative. I don't recommend investing by yourself. It's not a good strategy.

Another mistake people make when it comes to real estate investing is not understanding that you have to start small. A lot of people have monopoly in their head. They think that you have to start with a little greenhouse or start with residential property or flipping. Being a part of a community of experienced investors and having a mentor to help you get your 'real estate' game plan mapped out is imperative. By doing this, you can make quantum leaps. It's what got me from 2 doors to over 1,000 rental doors in just one year. I don't recommend investing without knowing what you're doing because there's a lot of money at stake. Ignorance is not bliss. Ignorance can be very costly.

Can you share an example of a woman you worked with who achieved great success?

Monick Halm: I have one client, a really incredible woman in Portland. She's a yoga teacher, and she and her husband wanted to start investing so that they could easily retire and leave something behind for her kids and grandkids. When she started with me, she and her husband were making decent incomes. She owned her own yoga studio, and he was an executive in a Fortune 500 company. She realized that she couldn't teach yoga forever, and when she and her husband stopped working, their income would pretty much stop too. She wanted to create passive income streams through real estate. She's been investing in real estate now for 3 years. They have 15 rental doors, and they've got enough passive income to replace her yoga studio income. She's escaped the rat race. Their goal is to keep investing until they have at least as much passive income to replace both her and her husband's income.

What inspired you to become a real estate investor and focus specifically on women?

Monick Halm: Believe it or not, I was more inspired partly by desperation. I was working as an attorney at the time and had a decent six-figure income; however, Los Angeles is so expensive that I couldn't afford to buy a house for myself. So, a friend and I bought a triplex together. We lived in one unit and rented out the other two.

Fast forward, I was miserable as an attorney. One day, my appendix ruptured, and I had to be immediately admitted to the hospital. The doctor said, "You're going to be here several days, and you're going to have at least 30 days at home to recover." My first thought was: *Oh, thank God. I don't have to go to work!* My second thought was: *This is not good! If being in the hospital with a life-threatening, excruciating illness is preferable to being at work, I need to change this.* I can 100% tell you that the appendicitis was caused by stress. It was my body telling me that my law job was literally killing me. I knew I had to make a change. That path of change led me to real estate. After I achieved my own real estate investing success, and seeing how male-dominated the real estate investing industry is, I decided to help women invest. I use my female gift of intuition. My style and tolerance for investing is different than most men. I know that is the case for many other women as well. So, I created the Real Estate Investor Goddesses Wealth Builders Program to teach women how to successfully invest in a way that honors their feminine nature.

Can you share a lesson that you learned early on that you still use today?

Monick Halm: What I learned early was to always pay attention to my intuition, to always listen to that still, small voice within. I learned that when I listened to that voice (even when it didn't seem to make any sense), I was happy with the results. It was that voice that guided me to real estate investing and where I am today. It's also the voice that told me the second I saw my husband that he was 'the one.'

On the other hand, when I ignored that voice, I was very unhappy with the results. I ignored that voice that told me, *before I even entered law school*, that it wouldn't be a happy path for me. That same voice told me not to take the job where I got appendicitis. That voice told me not to invest in my one real estate investment that has lost me money. I now consider myself a very intuitive person, and I have learned to always listen to my intuition.

What question should women who are interested in real estate investing ask themselves?

Monick Halm: I think there are a couple of questions that will be really helpful, but the most important question is: Why? Why do you want it? Because once you can tune in to your why, it could be really compelling. Examples of why are: "I want to leave a legacy for my kids" or "I want to get out of the rat race and replace my salary with passive income" or "I want to live my passion with a passive income and financial freedom" or "I want to be able to spend more time with my children and be there for them as they grow up." If your why is compelling enough, then you will do it. You'll take the steps that you need to take in order to get there. You'll get the education, and you'll take the actions, and you'll keep going even when it's hard.

In closing, what do you want to leave a woman with who either wants an additional stream of income, wants to change her career or wants to secure a comfortable retirement?

Monick Halm: You have the ability to invest in all sorts of real estate: residential, apartment buildings, mobile home parks, ground-up development projects and workforce housing, and medical office buildings. You can invest time, money, credit, or experience and get paid.

You have the ability to be a part of investments all across the country. We currently have property in California, Texas, Georgia, North Carolina, Louisiana, and New Mexico.

Working with the Real Estate Goddess Investors will allow you to begin to create a passive income, which means an income that you don't have to trade your time to get. Right now, most of you put in an hour, and you get a specific amount of time for that hour, or you might be on a salary. With real estate investing, you no longer are trading your time for money. Passive income is income that you always see regardless of whether or not you're working. You make money from cash flow, tenant rents and from the property appreciating (growing in value). You're receiving income even when you're sleeping or even when you're on vacation. It only makes sense to consider this revenue stream.

About Monick Halm

Monick Halm is a real estate investor, syndicator and developer with over 12 years of real estate investing experience in multi-family, mobile home parks, RV parks, flipping, vacation rentals, syndication, and ground-up development. Together with her husband and her investors, she owns over 1,200 rental units across 6 states.

She is the #1 bestselling author of *The Real Estate Investor Goddess Handbook* and the host of the "Real Estate Investor Goddesses" podcast. She is also a real estate investment strategy mentor, a *Huffington Post* contributing author, keynote speaker, recovered attorney, certified yoga teacher, certified interior designer, Feng Shui expert, avid world traveler, wife and mother of three amazing kids.

Monick earned her Juris Doctorate degree from Columbia Law School in New York and received a coach training certification from Coach Training Alliance. She has studied Reiki and attained the Reiki Master level. She has also studied the Law of Attraction Principles, Pleasure Living Principles, cognitive and behavioral sciences, positive psychology, and other modalities for living a healthier and more meaningful life.

Monick has made it her mission to empower women to thrive in their lives, families, and careers. She loves connecting with other real estate investing women.

WEBSITE
RealEstateInvestorGoddesses.com

FACEBOOK
Facebook.com/RealEstateInvestorGoddesses

TWITTER
Twitter.com/MonickPaulHalm

LINKEDIN
LinkedIn.com/in/MonickPaul

What it Takes to Get and Maintain Your Seat at the Boardroom Table – Wisdom from a Woman Who Has Sat at the Table with Titans

Do you have a seat at the table at your company? Are you an executive businesswoman, c-suite professional, or high-level manager running a thriving start-up or Fortune 100 company who finds herself in the boardroom with all men or desiring to have a seat at the boardroom table? Nicole Neal Armstrong can definitely relate. They say it's lonely at the top, but it doesn't have to be. C-suite and executive women face very different challenges than women in managerial positions and many times don't want to talk about or share those challenges, fears, and quite frankly, many times they don't know how to handle certain situations they find themselves in.

What if you could consult with and learn from a woman who raised $12 million in venture capital, was ranked #3 for fundraising by #ProjectDiane, who managed teams in excess of 600 employees, and who has been an integral part of very successful start-ups—one that went public and became a billion-dollar company and the other that was sold to Pearson, the largest education company in the world, for $250 million? Do you think she has faced some of the challenges you may be facing with your current seat or as you make your way to the top? And do you think you could glean some valuable nuggets from a woman with these achievements?

If you are ready to secure your seat at the table in your industry and want to receive private training from a woman who managed global teams (in India, Dubai, Paris, Belgium, Holland, Germany, and London), dined with billionaires in Dubai, managed P&Ls in excess of $50 million and has personally been responsible for double and triple digit growth at several companies, keep reading this chapter.

For the last 30 years, Nicole's engineer mind has built solutions and creatively solved problems so you don't have to stumble and struggle in your executive role. Nicole has a unique perspective and expertise to help women specifically maximize their individual and corporate performance. She is known as a transformational leader, and she 'leads from behind.' If you want access to someone that's been there and done that, you'll find Nicole Neal Armstrong's interview enlightening. –Conversation with Lisa C. Williams

Lisa Charlene Williams is the Founder of the #SmartHustle #SmartGrind movement (amiontheverge.com), an initiative to help female entrepreneurs succeed in business and life, stop working themselves to death and become the Doyennes of their industry, a woman who is the most respected or prominent person in a particular field.

Conversation with Nicole Neal Armstrong

You have achieved quite a bit of success! You were recently featured in Vanity Fair. You have a new book coming out. You have a consulting agency called Women to the Top. Can you share about all of that?

Nicole Neal Armstrong: Absolutely! I was honored when Vanity Fair reached out and said they wanted to pay homage to 26 women of color entrepreneurs/founders who had raised at least $1 million in venture capital. The likelihood of a woman of color successfully raising outside capital is less than 1%. It is great that Vanity Fair wanted to celebrate us in their April 2018 issue. Raising awareness around the inequities that we face is important.

I am also very excited about my book. I will share my years of experience at the table with titans, and I will share what it takes to get and maintain your seat at the table in your industry.

The book titled *In the Boardroom with Titans* chronicles my experience rising to the position of chief executive and all the things that I didn't know and had to learn. This is a great book for women who are at the top or trying to make their way there. I also think the book is a great read for college students and budding entrepreneurs, as it provides insight into why it is never too early to chart your path to success.

Women to the Top (WTTT) is an entrepreneurial endeavor near and dear to my heart. I started Women to the Top consulting with two other women. We started the consulting agency because we recognize that there aren't enough support structures for women executives and entrepreneurs. It is often lonely at the top, and we strongly believe that it doesn't have to be. We plan to kick-off WTTT with a series of retreats where we will focus on things like personal branding, dressing for success, boardroom training, prioritizing self and staying current with technologies that can improve business outcomes.

What are the advantages of hiring and consulting with a seasoned professional like you for an already accomplished executive woman?

Nicole Neal Armstrong: Well, I can tell you that experience is a great teacher. I can honestly say that I have 'been there' and 'done that.' Working with a seasoned professional like myself provides an accomplished executive woman with someone who really understands the stress that she faces. It provides her with a trusted advisor who will not judge her; will give her sound, actionable advice; will be strictly confidential; and will be solely focused on mapping her success.

What do you feel are the biggest myths about what it really takes to sustain a position in a Fortune 100 or 500 company and gain and keep respect at the boardroom table as a female?

Nicole Neal Armstrong: There are a lot of fallacies about what's required to stay at the top. I think the biggest myth is that when you reach the level of CEO, it is believed that you are at the top of the food chain and that you call all the shots. Not so much. The truth of the matter is that most organizations (this includes profit and not-for-profit organizations) have a governing body called a board. The CEO works for the board and is held accountable by the board. In essence, even as the chief executive, you often do not have the final say. White males heavily seat the majority of boards in the U.S. So, knowing the power that the board holds means that, as women, it is really critical that we learn how to build solid board relationships.

What are some common misconceptions about women in high salaried positions and their ability to contribute and be effective in the boardroom?

Nicole Neal Armstrong: I have noticed quite a few interesting misconceptions regarding women in high salaried positions. Women are thought to be emotional, unwilling to make tough decisions, and it is assumed there will be a struggle to understand the financial side of business. When you are in a boardroom, you must command respect. You absolutely need to be no-nonsense, but that doesn't mean you can't emote when necessary (but no crying allowed). There are often times when, as a woman executive, you need to make tough decisions like terminating an employee or shutting down operations. We are more than equipped to make these tough calls. Finally, knowing your numbers inside and out is an absolute must. It's been long believed that men are better at math than women. I strongly disagree, and if a woman does struggle in this area, there are plenty of online certificate courses that can help close the gap.

What are some of the most common fears executive women face at that level that many don't talk about?

Nicole Neal Armstrong: Admittedly, life at the top can be a real challenge for female executives. I can think of at least two common fears that executive women face.

1. They are afraid of making mistakes. The bar is really high for executive women. Their male counterparts are often given a lot of leeway if they don't get it right 'the first time.' The same is not true for women executives. We are often judged more harshly when targets are missed or ideas flop. As a result, one of the most common fears that executive women have is failure.

2. Women executives, especially those who are mothers, also fear that they will be viewed as being less committed than their male counterpart. Juggling the needs of a family is difficult, and if you need to take time off to care for your sick child, it is privately frowned upon.

How can they get past these fears?

Nicole Neal Armstrong: Let's tackle the fear of failure first. Every successful person knows that success is 99% failure. You must fail in order to succeed. I am certainly not suggesting that you make poorly informed decisions. What I am saying is that once you have a clear, well-thought strategy, you must take action. Push past the fear of failure and embrace the fact that you'll get more value out of learning what doesn't work than in doing nothing at all. Be thorough, decisive and own up to any mistakes you make.

As it relates to the pressures of being a mom, I say this: "Your 'presence' as a mother is more important than your presence as a woman executive." Do not apologize for taking care of your children, but make sure you don't abuse the time you need to take off. When possible, leverage babysitters and family to help. Again, it is worth repeating that you should not apologize for putting your children first. Now the truth of the matter is that you may have to burn the midnight oil once you get your children fed and tucked in bed, but that comes with the territory. If you want to 'have it all,' you must 'give your all.'

What are a few known pitfalls or common mistakes you see women make in upper-level positions?

Nicole Neal Armstrong: Wow! Well, there are quite a few mistakes I have witnessed. Some common mistakes include:

1. Underplaying their success.
2. Hiding their feminine side.
3. Detaching from other women.
4. Making poor hiring decisions.
5. Undervaluing the importance of mission and vision.
6. Creating a culture of fear and paranoia.

It is important for women to own their power if they ultimately want to be successful at a high level.

How can these pitfalls or mistakes be avoided?

Nicole Neal Armstrong: Let's take them one by one:

1. Underplaying their success. You don't have to make yourself decrease so that other people can increase and feel better about themselves. Remain humble but be proud of the hard work that you've done to get to where you are. Give yourself permission to shine.

2. Hiding their feminine side. You don't have to dress like the 'guys.' It's okay to wear skirts and high heels if that's your thing. Also, I am a firm believer that you should always dress for success. So, even if the office dress code is casual or business casual, you should always come to work put together. Always. Always.

3. Detaching from other women. As women, we must pull each other up. We don't have to be cutthroat, and we should not feel the need to separate ourselves from other women. Form bonds. You will find that these bonds are valuable and can come to your rescue when you least expect them to.

4. Making poor hiring decisions. Women have great gut instincts. The easiest way to derail a successful team is to make a toxic hire. If your 'spidey' senses go off about a potential hire, heed it and be as thorough as you can during the hiring process.

5. Undervaluing the importance of mission and vision. Misinformed employers believe that a person's salary is the most important factor in retaining talent. They are mistaken. The most important factor in retaining

talent is having a strong mission and vision. As mentioned previously, companies are comprised of people. People are innately motivated by common goals. Make sure you invest a good amount of time in aligning everyone to the company's mission.

6. Creating a culture of fear and paranoia. When you create an environment where people are afraid to contribute, afraid to make mistakes and afraid to think on their own, you have created an organization that will inevitably fail. Employees need to feel safe, and they are most invigorated when they are encouraged to take risks. This is tied back to that fear of failure. Don't be afraid to fail and encourage your team to be innovative. You'll be pleasantly surprised at the outcome.

Can you share an example of how you have helped a female executive overcome an obstacle and achieve her desired outcome?

Nicole Neal Armstrong: Yes! I have a fond memory of helping a young lady and was grateful for the opportunity to support her. The young woman I worked with was an exceptional manager but had no formal training in financial management. I worked with this young woman every week for six months and taught her everything I knew about P&L management. My proudest moment was when she was able to train her second in command on the techniques that she learned from me. I eventually left the organization, and the young women left about a year after I did. She was able to secure an even more senior level position because of her command of business financials.

What inspired you to shift from running and creating highly profitable start-ups to start your own consultancy?

Nicole Neal Armstrong: Well, I learned more about myself in the four years I served as CEO than I did my entire career. There were great highs and lots of lows. As I reflected on that experience, I knew that I would have greatly benefited from having someone to talk to, someone who really understood what I was going through. I started my own consultancy because I want to help women by providing them with the tools and know how to get to the top and stay there.

Can you share a lesson you learned early on that still impacts how you do business today?

Nicole Neal Armstrong: Of course! One of the earliest lessons I learned is that people, not systems or processes, build companies. It is critical that you develop authentic relationships with your team. If you invest in building up your team, creating a safe space for learning and growing and making sure they understand and are excited about the mission, nothing is impossible. Nothing.

What would you say to an executive woman if she desires to advance at her company and obtain a decision-maker seat at the table?

Nicole Neal Armstrong: For me, it's very clear. If you are an executive woman, and you desire to advance at your company, you have to be excellent. Period. My favorite quote is by Aristotle: "We are what we repeatedly do. Excellence then is not an act but a habit." Being on time for every meeting, responding promptly to important emails, meeting or beating deadlines, and making sure the quality of your work is exceptional are just a few ways to establish yourself as an outstanding employee.

Furthermore, if you want to obtain a seat at the table, you must get up every day and ask yourself three things: 1) *How can I exceed expectations on every task I am given?* 2) *Am I building the right relationships at the top level?* Trust me, getting a seat at the table is 70% who you know and 30% what you know/how you perform. Take key stakeholders out to lunch. Get to know the name of their wives, their children, their likes and dislikes. 3) *Am I viewed as a trusted leader and a walking example of someone who imbibes the mission and the vision of the organization?*

What's the most important question a female executive should think about to determine if hiring an executive coach would enhance her career?

Nicole Neal Armstrong: I believe there are a few that should be asked. The most important questions a female executive should think about are: Do you have a trusted partner who you can talk to when you are really unsure of the best course of action to take? Are you talking to someone who has been where you are and who won't judge you when you share your insecurities? Are there still things that you feel you have to learn and who are you learning from? Are you investing in your own personal growth and development, or are you leaving that up to your company?

What would you like to leave corporations with, and what is the benefit they will receive working with you?

Nicole Neal Armstrong: I love to inspire. I would like to leave corporations with the confidence that regardless of the obstacles they face, they can make it. If you can find a partner or a senior advisor who has the requisite experience to help you navigate and triage the roadblocks, your probability of 'making it' greatly increases. You cannot be afraid or too proud to seek help. The benefit corporations will receive in working with me is that I have 25+ years of solid experience working for large and small companies. My intuition and business acumen are exceptional from both a strategy and execution standpoint.

How can someone find out more about you, Nicole, and Women to the Top?

Nicole Neal Armstrong: You can find out more about me by visiting my LinkedIn page, reading my upcoming book *In the Boardroom with Titans* and visiting my website: www.takingwomentothetop.com.

About Nicole Neal Armstrong

Nicole Neal Armstrong started coding when she was 11-years-old and hasn't stopped pioneering since. She is a visionary leader who has been a part of three successful start-ups. Two of those start-ups had successful exits. One went public and became a billion-dollar company, and the other was sold to Pearson, the largest education company in the world, for $250 million. Nicole was the chief architect and visionary for an education technology start-up that she co-founded called Noodle Markets (www.noodlemarkets.com). She led the company in its mission to build a market network that creates efficacy and transparency within the K-12 purchasing landscape and raised $12 million in venture capital for it. This led her to be ranked as #3 in terms of fundraising by #ProjectDiane—an achievement quite rare for an African American female.

Prior to co-founding Noodle Markets, Nicole was the President of the Education Solutions Group at CORE Education

Consulting and Solutions LLC, a publicly traded company. Nicole managed a portfolio of formative assessment, intervention, teacher substitute management and content solutions for districts and states serving the Pre-K, K-12, Employability, Special Education, and Higher Education sectors. Nicole also served as the Senior Vice President of Major Accounts and State Services for Pearson Education Inc., one of the world's largest education publishing and technology companies. Prior to Pearson, she served as Senior Vice President of Client Services for Schoolnet Inc., where she played an important part in driving the company's accelerated growth, leading to Pearson's acquisition of Schoolnet.

Nicole graduated with honors and holds a Bachelor of Science in Computer Engineering from Binghamton University's Watson School of Engineering. She earned a Master of Business Administration, with distinction, from the University of Maryland University College. Nicole is a master at transforming organizations, developing high performing teams, cultivating leaders at various stages of their professional growth and imbibing a culture of excellence with every company she's helped grow.

WEBSITE
TakingWomenToTheTop.com

www.ingramcontent.com/pod-product-compliance
Lightning Source LLC
Chambersburg PA
CBHW060606210326
41519CB00014B/3587